'Existing in the middle of forces we only partially participants in an unfolding mystery of the human journey from MD to DD . In our desire to make a difference from our personal positions in systems, we create for ourselves illusions of power and authority; illusions that can both liberate and imprison us. *Managing Without Power* offers a wealth of concepts with which to winnow out the "liberators" from the "imprisoners"'.
— **John Bazalgette**, *co-founder of the Grubb Institute of Behavioral Studies, based in London, UK*

'This book invites us to question existing ideas about power so as to consider the capacity of power. Through deepening Steiner's work, the authors offer organizational leaders' insights into how the dynamics and influence of power can be the catalyst for positive and collaborative change'.
— **Dr. Mandy Lacy**, *TSTA-O, is a consultant, coach, and educator working in New Zealand*

'Often we see power through a negative frame, identified with authority and control over others. Anne de Graaf and Klaas Kunst invite us to re-think that metaphor, to actively choose a language of power based on passion, knowledge, communication, and love, to frame it as a positive and mutual capacity to bring transformation'.
— **Trudi Newton**, *award-winning writer and educator in the field of Transactional Analysis, UK*

'*Managing Without Power* is anything but another management book with tricks and treats. This book by Anne de Graaf and Klaas Kunst is like a mirror and critical friend for all leaders who want to continuously develop as a human being and as a professional. A timeless book, insensitive to hype'.
— **Albert Jansen**, *former chairman of the BMC group, a leading consultancy firm for the public sector in The Netherlands*

'This book is grounded in the work of Claude Steiner, an important voice in TA history, who developed a model of seven sources of healthy power. The authors extend Steiner's concepts and apply them with care and finesse in a variety of management tasks. Although the book is written with a focus on organizational management, it transcends that focus. In today's troubled world, this is a timely book – one might say urgent'.
— **William F. (Bill) Cornell**, *an author, a practicing TA therapist and trainer; consulting editor to the Transactional Analysis Journal; and editor of the Innovation in Transactional Analysis book series. He lives and works in the United States*

'The content of this book confirms that "knowledge is power" by offering intellectual and provocative elaborations with accessible application to diverse contexts around the world. I felt empowered with quality information when reflecting on power relations in the workplace, in the social, political, and economic dynamics of the country where I live, Brazil'.

—**Michelle Thomé**, *Transactional Analyst, certified by Unat-Brasil. She lives and works in Brazil.*

Managing Without Power

Largely inspired by the work of the American social psychologist Dr. Claude Steiner and the theory of Transactional Analysis, this book explores alternatives to power and how we can use these to work and manage more effectively, with integrity and joy.

Within this book, the authors examine and expand on Steiner's idiosyncratic views on the role of 'power' in our lives and work, which led to a new view of the relationship between management and power. Steiner suggested seven alternative ways to be influential, without the use of power, which include: grounding, passion, control, empathy/love, communication, knowledge, and transcendence. This book explores and describes these seven alternative sources of power in more detail, and how they can be used to produce change and increase the personal power of all, rather than playing power games.

This will be a valuable resource for managers and leaders in all types of organizations, as well as for coaches, clinicians, and anyone who is interested in forms of influence other than the use of (autocratic) power.

Anne de Graaf (MSc) is TSTA in the field of management and organizational development and CTA in the field of psychotherapy. Anne was founder, trainer, and supervisor at the Dutch TA academy and was a lecturer at the MSc Organizational TA program in the UK. He is currently the owner of RondHeel, consultancy and training. He is a coauthor of *Into TA: A Comprehensive Textbook on Transactional Analysis* and of *Einstein and the Art of Sailing*. He also coedited *Climate Change in Organizations* and *New Theory and Practice of Transactional Analysis in Organizations*.

Klaas Kunst pursued a degree in Dutch linguistics and literature. After working as a teacher and counselor at a secondary school, he transitioned into a senior consultant role and later assumed the position of a managing director within a governmental organization. Collaborating with his colleague Anne de Graaf, he coauthored several management books, one of which is *Einstein and the Art of Sailing*. In his private practice, his primary focus lies on providing individual and team coaching services.

Managing Without Power

Seven Alternative Ways
to be Influential

Anne de Graaf and Klaas Kunst

Routledge
Taylor & Francis Group

LONDON AND NEW YORK

First published 2024
by Routledge
4 Park Square, Milton Park, Abingdon, Oxon OX14 4RN

and by Routledge
605 Third Avenue, New York, NY 10158

Routledge is an imprint of the Taylor & Francis Group, an informa business

British Library Cataloguing-in-Publication Data
A catalogue record for this book is available from the British Library

Library of Congress Cataloging-in-Publication Data
Names: Graaf, Anne de, 1951– author. | Kunst, Klaas, author.
Title: Managing without power : seven alternative ways to be influential / Anne
    de Graaf and Klaas Kunst.
Description: Abingdon, Oxon ; New York, NY : Routledge, 2024. | Includes
    bibliographical references and index.
Identifiers: LCCN 2023058508 (print) | LCCN 2023058509 (ebook) | ISBN
    9781032589718 (hardback) | ISBN 9781032589701 (paperback) | ISBN
    9781003452386 (ebook)
Subjects: LCSH: Communication in management. | Influence (Psychology) |
    Management—Psychological aspects.
Classification: LCC HD30.3 .G69 2024 (print) | LCC HD30.3 (ebook) |
    DDC 658.4/5—dc23/eng/20240226
LC record available at https://lccn.loc.gov/2023058508
LC ebook record available at https://lccn.loc.gov/2023058509

ISBN: 978-1-032-58971-8 (hbk)
ISBN: 978-1-032-58970-1 (pbk)
ISBN: 978-1-003-45238-6 (ebk)

DOI: 10.4324/9781003452386

Typeset in Times New Roman
by Apex CoVantage, LLC

Contents

About this book

This book is for anyone who wants to explore how to work with power effectively without constant recourse to positional or personal power. This book is for anyone who want to explore how to work with integrity and joy. But this book is also, for those in a position in which exercising hierarchical power is not a realistic option. Finally, this book is for all those readers who want to use their personal qualities more to exert optimal influence.

The message of this book is not that managing with power (control of many by few) is by definition wrong everywhere and always. Managing without power however appears to be a serious option that is worth exploring. In that sense, this book is a quest that we would like to embark on together with all readers. Great leaders who steered by inner beacons have led the way of management without power in world history. Nelson Mandela once sighed, "The problem is not that I don't know how to use my power. The problem is that I don't know how not to use that power.'

The content of this book is largely inspired by the work of the American social psychologist Dr. Claude Steiner. At the end of the last century, he wrote a groundbreaking article about the role of 'power' in our lives and work. Steiner's idiosyncratic view led to a new view of the relationship between management and power. The biggest advantage of his approach is that the seven sources of power from his ideas considerably increase the personal power of all. And that's good news!

Happy reading,
Anne de Graaf and Klaas Kunst

Recommendation
(written for the Dutch edition
of this book)

I've been intrigued by the dynamics of power for all my life. In 1987, I wrote an article for the *Transactional Analysis Journal*: 'The seven sources of power, an alternative to authority'. The first sentence of that article, 'Power is almost universally and mistakenly seen as the capacity to control others', was the theme of *The Other Side of Power: How to Become Powerful Without Being Power-Hungry* (1981), a book in which I explore the proper use as well as the abuse of power in our world. In my recent book, *The Heart of the Matter, Love, Information & Transactional Analysis* (2009), you can read further refinements in my thinking about this most important subject.

I am very happy that Anne de Graaf and Klaas Kunst, who are both advocates for Transactional Analysis, took up the challenge to further the dialogue about the seven sources of power. The world of management and leadership needs to keep on reflecting on the use of power. Without such reflection, abuse is around the corner. I define power as 'the capacity to produce change', hopefully change for the better – a better organizational climate in which both managers and employees can give their very best. It is my belief that people are most effective when they exercise their heart-centered, individual powers in cooperative concert with each other. This book provides much information to that end.

Dr. Claude Steiner
Berkeley, California, USA, summer 2009

Transactional Analysis: what is it?

Ideas from Transactional Analysis (TA) are regularly used in this book. On this page, you can read briefly what TA is about. A few concepts from the TA that are used several times are also explained by the authors.

Transactional Analysis (TA) is a theory about personality, communication, and change, developed in the 1950s and 1960s. The founder of Transactional Analysis is the Canadian psychiatrist Dr. Eric Berne (1910–1970). Berne was a pioneer and radical thinker in psychiatry. He developed this deep and systematic theory to enable personal development and healthy relationships.

Belief in self-responsibility and in the self-management capacity of people are the pillars underpinning the thinking and doing of the TA. The TA offers a practical, clear theory that can be understood by everyone. It is a model that makes manageable the complexity and depth of yourself, your relationships, and the groups and organizations in which you live and work.

A few TA concepts referred to in this book are as follows:

Ego states

Patterns can often be recognized in people's behavior, which can be directly traced back to the five different so-called ego states: Structuring Parent (SP), Nurturing Parent (NP), Adult (A), Natural Child (NC), and Adapted Child (AC).

Script

Script is described as the unconscious life plan with which people shape their lives and which the young child decides on as a result of parental programming and childhood experiences. Each of us creates an explanatory story in the first years of life. It provides us with a script for tackling problems in the present. And it predicts the future. We all write the story of our lives.

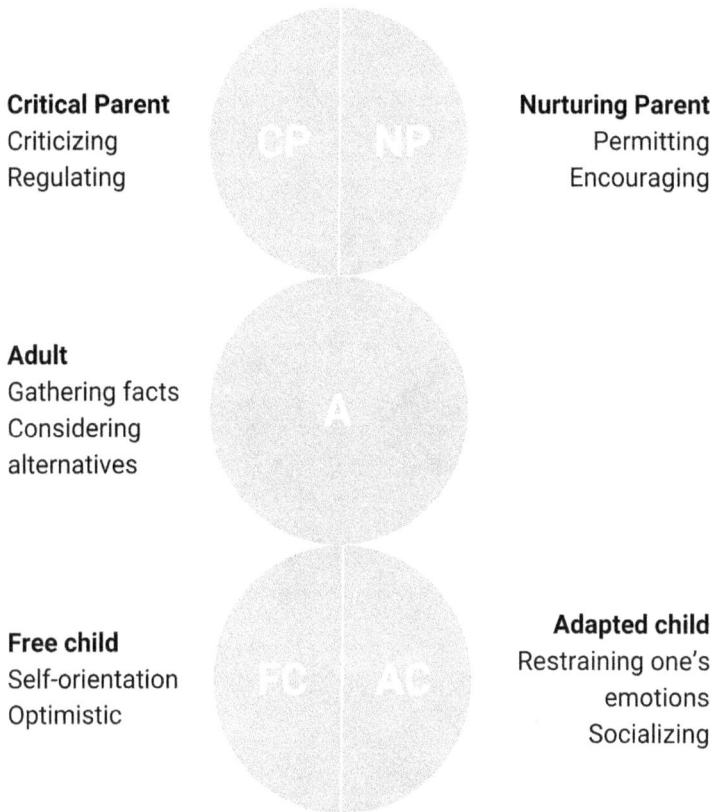

Critical Parent
Criticizing
Regulating

Nurturing Parent
Permitting
Encouraging

Adult
Gathering facts
Considering
alternatives

Free child
Self-orientation
Optimistic

Adapted child
Restraining one's
emotions
Socializing

Strokes

Within Transactional Analysis (TA), we use the word stroke to indicate 'a unit of recognition'. Strokes are vital – so vital that people would rather be scolded than overlooked. In short, negative strokes are better than no strokes at all. Strokes come in different shapes and sizes.

Anyone who wants to know more about Transactional Analysis can consult the book, published by Routledge in 2016, *Into TA: A Comprehensive Textbook on Transactional Analysis*, edited by William F. Cornell, Anne de Graaf, Trudi Newton, and Moniek Thunnissen.

1 You cannot not have an impact

Influence or be influenced?

It is said that a visitor once came to the home of Nobel-Prize-winning physicist Niels Bohr. Having noticed a horseshoe hung above the entrance, he asked incredulously if the professor believed horseshoes brought good luck. 'No', Bohr replied, 'but I am told that they bring luck even to those who do not believe in them' (www.laphamsquarterly.org/magic-shows/miscellany/niels-bohrs-lucky-horseshoe, approached on April 5, 2023).

This book takes you on a journey, like in the anecdote about Bohr, along what is believed about 'what works and what doesn't work'. The theme of power is consciously, but much more unconsciously, peppered with countless presuppositions, assumptions, prejudices, and beliefs. We all hold beliefs about 'how power works and how power doesn't work'. One of the funniest definitions of power we came across while researching this book is by Michael Korda (1991) and reads: 'Power is the extent to which you can make others wait for you as opposed to having you wait for them'. Of course, the definition isn't just funny. Power often works just like that!

In this book, we invite you to question existing ideas about 'how power works and how power doesn't work'. We are happy to take you with us on our search for the possibilities and impossibilities of power. We intend to ask curious questions to start a conversation about congealed and sometimes rusted in ideas. And occasionally, we formulate a tentative position of our own. Bohr probably leaves his visitor confused by saying, 'It seems to work even if you don't believe in it'. That is also what we aim for: To create a little confusion in the mind about 'power', so that there is room for a new view of the possibilities and impossibilities of the use of power. We join the saying: 'Confusion means you're about to learn something' (Seminar Tony Robbins, Brussels 1995).

Words of power

Power has a rather negative and often masculine connotation. In conversations about power, abuse of power, lust for power, word of power, power

DOI: 10.4324/9781003452386-1

struggle, and display of power are often discussed. Power seems strongly linked to dominance and superiority. Power, you might say, has a bad reputation. If you look at it more neutrally, you can see that the meaning of power is closer to words such as 'strength', 'potency', or 'capacity'. For example, think of words like empowerment and horsepower. Power also indicates, for example in the manual of many devices, whether something is 'on' or 'off'. You can turn power on or off. There is nothing wrong with that.

'Language is power', as the French philosopher Michel Foucault wrote in The order of things (1966). We use language, the words we choose, to create a reality for ourselves and for others. Anyone who systematically says that 'love is a battlefield' should not be surprised if their own relationships and those of others are dominated by occasional or regular fights. Managers would do well to be sharp and alert to their use of language. They define the reality of their company for their employees who will behave as they think that reality requires of them.

After all, language is more than just the exchange of information (Steens, 1993). Language is also a form of influence: verbal and nonverbal. No one can escape that! The influence we exert on others externally through the language we use is experienced by them internally. And vice versa. What we observe is only the outside: behavior that takes shape in communication. Our inside – feelings, intentions, experiences, meanings, and thoughts – guides how we interpret the language used. That inside is not directly known and accessible to the other. What our exterior produces on the other is the intended or unintended effect. The other is the other side for us. So, with our inside, we interpret through the outside of the other what may be going on inside. It is no wonder that communication is sometimes difficult . . .

Claude Steiner

The theme for this book was inspired by an article published late last century and written by Claude Steiner (1935–2017), one of the coworkers of Eric Berne (1910–1970). Berne is the founder of the Transactional Analysis (TA) model. TA is a theory of personality, communication, and change, which examines communication between people and the underlying dynamic (drivers and stoppers) and patterns. TA focuses on the interdependence of intra- and interpersonal processes and of group processes, embedded in a larger whole. Steiner wrote a contribution to the *Transactional Analysis Journal* (TAJ) in 1987 entitled 'The seven sources of power: An alternative to authority'. In that article, he places a series of critical comments on the self-evidence, with which people take hierarchy and dominance for granted. In relationships, families, organizations and companies, societies, and even on a global scale, we almost seem to take power and impotence as a natural phenomenon. Steiner does not believe in the inevitability of power and rejects the idea that we must accept it in our life and work. To investigate to what extent this thinking about power is caused by a belief system that has already been developed in childhood, he introduces the TA concept 'script'.

Script (Berne, 1963) is a central concept in Transactional Analysis. In short, sometimes, it seems as if there is a common thread running through all the events of your life. It then seems as if an invisible plan directs your life. In TA, that common thread is called your 'script'. Your script is your best attempt to make sense of what you observed and experienced when you were a small child. Your script basically answers the question: What is someone like me doing with people like you in a world like this? In the words of Richard Erskine (1980):

> Life scripts are a complex set of unconscious relational patterns based on physiological survival reactions, implicit experiential conclusions, explicit decisions, and/or self-regulating introjections, made under stress, at any developmental age, that inhibit spontaneity and limit flexibility in problem-solving, health maintenance, and in relationship with people.

Children are in a one-down position with respect to their parents, who are in a one-up position. The lessons learned in the early years are used later in life by people to 'stay in control' and thus maintain or improve their situation. 'Power games', mocks Steiner.

Seven sources

A syndrome related to power is 'hybris': the Greek term for excessive pride or self-confidence. Many leaders suffer from this. The reason is that they, because of their leading role, run the risk of becoming increasingly isolated. The healthy feedback from their immediate environment threatens to disappear, which increases their blind spot. The first line of defense against hybris is correction by a partner or by children, extended family, and friends. But even that is sometimes lacking. And if the working environment does not correct either, drama is lurking for the 'subjects'. Some people will do anything to make a powerful impression. Steiner writes (p. 102): 'Power is almost universally and mistakenly seen as the capacity to control other people. Here it is defined as the capacity to produce change'. In his article in *Transactional Analysis Journal*, he then explores seven other ways to exert influence – to bring about change without 'bossing' about other people:

- Being grounded
- Passion
- Empathy
- Control
- Communication
- Information
- Transcendence

In this book, we accompany Steiner on his quest. His article is an inspiration to us. In this book, we further deepen his ideas and broaden them here and there. Above all, we want to make his ideas applicable to the practice of every manager. It is and was a special treasure hunt.

Too much or too little

Each source of power can be underdeveloped to the point of nonexistence or overdeveloped so that it crowds out other sources of power, Steiner writes (p. 103). Ofman (2001) shows that people always run the risk of using too much or too little of their qualities. In both cases, they sell themselves short. When too much of a quality (power source) is used, Ofman speaks of a pitfall, where the quality has a negative effect on the environment and also forms an obstacle for the person in question. The source of power gets distorted. Insufficient use of a quality (source of power) also has negative consequences for the environment and for the person in question. In that case, it is important to investigate what challenge there is to ensure that available quality (source of power) is used properly.

By recognizing qualities (sources of power) in oneself and one's employees, managers can create environments that allow individuals to flourish within organizations. So, all seven sources of power are at risk of not having the impact they could have. Just as well as all seven of them can make a difference in company and organization. We will dwell on this in each chapter.

Manager: *manu agere*?!

The word manager has its origin in Latin: *manu agere*. That literally means 'take someone by the hand'. That looks a lot like a form of management, fitting in with a hierarchical organizational principle! It suits companies that declare shareholder value sacrosanct and see employees merely as a means to achieve that goal through their managers. Directing and controlling employees then become a foreground in the behavior of the manager. You just have to take them by the hand.

If you have to take someone by the hand, it is obvious that you place that other person in a relationship of dependency, telling him 'I'm OK, you're not OK (yet)'. The risk is that the employee will display dependent behavior, leading to passivity, an accommodating attitude, and a lack of personal responsibility and creativity. It then seems that there is only one 'best way', namely that of the manager. The manager has the sole right to represent the Parent in the organization. The Parent knows what is good for the Children. The manager also has the sole right to make mature decisions about the progress of work. The employees do not have many rights, especially in the role of Adapted Children, and have to do what the manager wants them to do.

If we use the term manager in this book, we prefer not to opt for the '*manu agere* variant'. It is mainly characterized by one-way traffic, by strength and figures and percentages. It's no wonder that many employees don't feel taken seriously by this type of manager. Especially the moral aspect of the work remains underexposed. On the work floor, this is felt and experienced as: this is not about us! For many, this leads to underperformance and is ultimately not as efficient as thought . . . If we introduce the manager here, then that role stands for a leader who inspires, informs, who integrates the soft and hard side of the work, who assumes reciprocity, who exudes authority and respects his employees, takes them seriously, and trusts and allows for autonomy.

In 1989, it was Quinten Holdeman who gave this method of setting up a management agent of the name symbiotic chain. The symbiotic chain symbol represents the extension of social interdependency downward through one to several levels of supervision within a company. The chain's effect is that it isolates top management from the creative and innovative ideas of autonomous individuals at the shopfloor level. The chain's impact on promotion creates a paucity of leadership-in-depth in the workplace by reducing the probability of promotion of autonomous individuals. Autonomy is not appreciated!

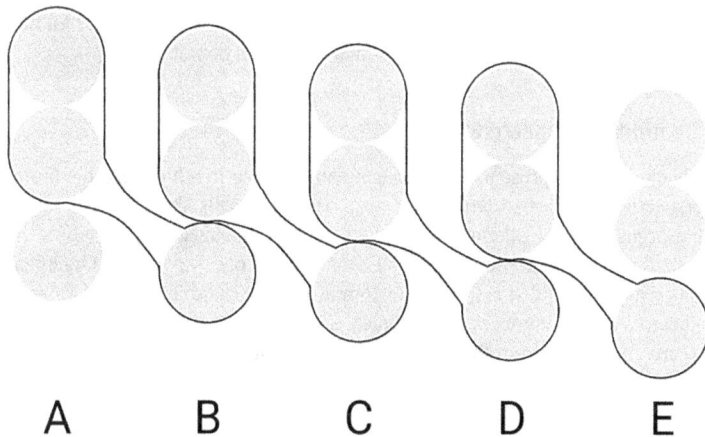

Figure 1.1 Symbiosis in organizations

Autocratic power

It appears that nowadays, more countries are governed by an autocratic leader (dictator) than by a leader elected democratically. Autocracy seems to be the rule rather than the exception. Jacobs (1987), in his award-winning article, notes that autocratic rulers have the tendency to oversimplify both problems and solutions. They also seem to put more energy in capturing people's hearts than their minds. Jacobs is intrigued by the question of how leaders and followers form a movement that eventually oppresses others. Mind boggling. An important question here is: What is the role of the bystanders while this is going on? To set up a system that is controlled by autocratic power, you need masters, followers, and . . . bystanders.

Ultimately in the master–follower symbiosis, individuation is no longer possible. The chain (Figure 1.1) becomes self-evident. Tragedy appears inevitable.

Jacobs is clear when he notes that fear forms the basis of the relationship between master and follower and that fear also neutralizes the will to intervene among many bystanders. Masters present themselves as having the answer, the solution to all the people's fears. This induces dependency in followers. History shows that in the end, the master is riddled with hubris, arrogance, hostility, and control coercion. They know, as they repeatedly say, what should happen after a natural disaster, an economic downturn, a match carelessly thrown in a haystack, a shift in the wind, a baby's cry – events that confront people with the fact that they do not have everything under control. So, plenty of opportunities for autocrats!

In an article previously published by us on the role of the bystander (1998), we show that the largest group in autocratically controlled systems is the group of bystanders. Bystanders remain passive and give permission by saying nothing and doing nothing. We would like to close this short section on autocratic power with the famous quote from Edmond Burke (1816): 'All that is necessary for the triumph of evil is that good men do nothing'.

The moral perspective

This chain also represents the management thinking in which also the moral perspective remains underexposed and, moreover, falls short in many complex organizational dilemmas. If the role of the manager is seen only in its original sense, this invites superficial behavior and one-way traffic. Organizations with a one-sided emphasis on formal and measurable key performance indicators (KPIs: numbers, percentages, and euros) especially demand strong directive behavior from their managers. That is not always necessarily undesirable. They are in the danger of forgetting that other tasks are at least as important for achieving good results such as:

- Keeping people inspired
- Keeping people informed

- Keeping people involved
- Keeping people interested

These are indicators that take note of employees' commitment and involvement, that are based on their basic benevolence, and that align with people's intrinsic motivation to contribute. Managers should invite employees to bring all three ego states (Parent, Adult, Child) to work. Such a working method actually leads to more involvement, stronger motivation, and growing attachment of employees to (the goals of) the organization and to each other. In the end, value-oriented purposefulness wins out over measurable effectiveness.

Scripted beliefs

In this first chapter, we invite you to start thinking about power at the beginning: yourself! It describes how a manager who regularly finds himself in difficult situations knows one thing for sure: the constant factor in all those situations is 'me, myself and I'. At least I have myself under control, don't I? It becomes clear that (personal) beliefs about power all too easily become dominant in the daily practice of the manager. A manager who thinks he must make regular use of his (formal or objective) power will eventually weaken his possibilities to exert influence. Thinking about and acting from power (or impotence) are rooted in our early childhood experiences. Our (scripted) beliefs about how 'power and impotence' work reflect our early childhood strategies for exerting influence. The 'will to power' was introduced into psychology by the Austrian psychiatrist Alfred Adler (1924) to indicate the need, especially in men, to outdo and dominate others. An idea is central to his thinking is that when young children feel that they have no place in the system in which they grow up and cannot contribute, they will try to overcome feelings of inferiority through a pursuit of superiority, based on a misguided belief. Again, this book about power finds its starting point in the preliminary work done by Claude Steiner. Every chapter starts with a few sentences about his thinking in relation to that specific source of influence.

A complex force field

Why does one manager go through life whistling happily, while the other eventually collapses? Why does one feel like a fish in water, while the other succumbs to powerlessness and despondency? Of course, managers are under great pressure from time to time, if only because of the constant compulsion to perform. But there's more. Managers must deal with a complex field of forces and power. Think of 'the upward pressure' of their team or department and 'the downward pressure' of the management team or the board. Their own team expects the manager to represent the interests of the team in board meetings. The management expects the same manager to represent the interests of the organization to his people. Middle managers often are in the corner where the blows fall. The middle manager is seen as someone who is stuck in 'the sandwich'. An example from practice: a manager is completely stuck in the sandwich between team and management. For a while he still has saved face by suggesting to his team that it is very difficult to wheel and deal with this board. But now he doesn't see how he can exert influence anymore, feels powerless, and decides to leave. In a final interview with the general manager, he is taken aback and says that half of the people in this team do not meet the minimum requirements of willingness and ability. It can't both be true, can it? Sometimes a man can't see a way out! The main stressors for middle managers are the lack of control over the primary process and the lack of support from upper management. Stress and fun factors too often appear to be out of balance in the daily work of the middle manager. The public sector and the business community benefit from well-motivated (they must want to) and well-trained (they must also be able to) managers – managers who can take a beating! For the record: although the middle manager is often seen as a sandwich manager, another perspective is also possible: the middle managers are in the exceptionally unique position that they can influence both ways, using all their qualities.

There is of course a lot of diversity among managers: older and younger; women and men; differences in cultural background and religion; years of experience; and starting, part-timers, and full-timers. All these characteristics can help answer the question 'why one perseveres and the other drops out'. It is our experience that only difference in experience and difference in age explain the degree of sensitivity to stress to some extent. But there is much more to it!

Attribution

In research (Weiner, 1985) into psychological factors of stress sensitivity, the concept of 'causal attribution' is introduced. This involves the question of what people themselves see as the reasons for achieving or not achieving a certain goal. Causes that cannot be influenced are more likely to lead to feelings of powerlessness than causes that can be tackled. At the extremes of the spectrum, the following instructive picture can be seen: managers with a so-called negative attribution pattern experience considerably more stress and less pleasure than their colleagues with a positive attribution pattern.

• Negative attribution pattern

Managers with a negative attribution pattern place the causes of perceived stress outside of themselves. They also often believe that those causes are permanent and cannot be influenced by them. Demotivation and lack of satisfaction are the obvious consequences of this attribution pattern: 'This team is beating a dead horse!' or 'This management will never work here!'

• Positive attribution pattern

These managers look for the causes of perceived tension, which can change all the time, including themselves. They have sufficient control over the situations in which these causes can be of influence. And, unlike the first group, they are hardly bothered by feelings of despondency and powerlessness: 'I am always looking for ways to improve sharpness in my team and how I can set an example of this myself.'

Ever since Karpman's (1971) award-winning article entitled 'Options', the theme of options has regularly reappeared in TA literature. Very often, people who seek the help of another, in the private world or in the professional world, are stuck because they ran out of options. They see no other possibilities than the possibilities they have already tried. Limitations caused by their script obviously play an important role here.

Three options

They need to learn to deal with an old principle that allows for three options only. This principle shows that in undesirable situations, every person always has three options (de Graaf, 2022):

• Accept

Determine what is changeable and what is not and then make the choice (!) to accept what is not changeable: 'I think, after careful consideration, that I am not the person who can lead this change. I agree that Peter will take care of this', or 'The grid has been carefully put together and, although I'm not happy about it, I'm going to make the best of it'.

• Change

Determine what is changeable and what is not and then put time and energy into what is changeable: 'It has to happen at the start of the calendar year. I will certainly not pass up this opportunity. And I'm counting on your cooperation, too', or 'I refuse to accept that our department wouldn't be able to deliver on time. They did it in previous situations too!'

• Say goodbye

Determining what is changeable and what is not to say goodbye if acceptance and change are not desirable or possible: 'The agreements that have now been finalized regarding the identity of our institute do not suit me. I now choose to leave', or 'If there are no more opportunities for me to develop further here, I will go one step further'.

With attribution, it is therefore important to name your own share and to be able to estimate its value – positively or not. Asking the question: how am I part of this myself? While this may seem unappealing and uncomfortable, it is precisely this approach that makes it happen that you can take control again, that your sense of influence increases. Because one thing is certain: you have some control over your own change, and you only have a very limited say in the change in your environment!

Self-fulfilling prophecy

You know the joke about the company that only knew two rules: Rule 1 – the boss is always right! Rule 2 – if the boss is not right, rule 1 automatically comes into effect. A joke? Many managers' thinking about their role is strongly influenced by their beliefs about power and how power works. In this paragraph, we look for answers to the question of how (strong) beliefs influence a stamp on (experienced) reality.

Within Transactional Analysis, the concept of the so-called 'racket system' (Erskine and Zalcman, 1979) is helpful. Julie Hay (2009) calls it 'an inner, self-perpetuating system that connects our beliefs, our actions, and our reinforcements'. The racket system actually describes the psychological pattern behind a self-fulfilling prophecy. A manager with the conviction 'If I don't say loud and clear what needs to be done, nothing will happen' can get it confirmed (reinforced) every day. His behavior will be fed by this conviction on a social (verbal) level and especially on a psychological (nonverbal) level. The reactions of his employees (especially to his nonverbal signals) will strengthen him in this belief. In a diagram, the racket system (also called script cycle) looks like what is given in Figure 1.2.

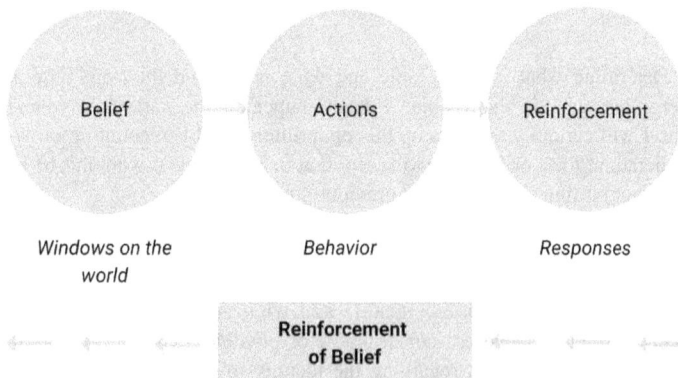

Figure 1.2 Self-fulfilling prophecy

Beliefs

In his first book on Transactional Analysis, writing about TA vocabulary, Berne coined the concept of 'script' and 'script beliefs' (Berne, 1961). This is about beliefs that we hold about ourselves, the other, and the world/life. Many of these are based on our early childhood experiences. Remember that children do not think like adults (Bradshaw, 1990). Children's thinking is often magical, illogical, egocentric, and absolutistic. Children believe that certain words, gestures, or behaviors can change reality: 'I upset my mother!' (magical thinking). Children regularly reason emotionally: 'I feel guilty, so I am a bad person' (illogical thinking). Children personalize almost everything: 'If my father insists on his own way instead of listening to me, there must be something wrong with me' (egocentric thinking). Children tend to think in an all-or-nothing polarity: 'If my father enforces his will, all men will do so' (absolutistic thinking). Later, we take a closer look at what most children learn about power. Script beliefs begin to act as glasses and a filter for the reality in which we live and work. What we have come to believe about how power works determines which experiences we pay attention to. Our beliefs also influence how we subsequently interpret those experiences. The weight we give to it comes from the world of our beliefs. Let's ask the manager who now says 'But surely it is so!' to think about the aphorism 'A fact is something like a belief that we don't want to change'!

Actions

Our scripted beliefs color our (racket) behavior and thus influence how we express our feelings, what words we use, the tone of our voice, our body posture, and more. The manager for whom it is the most normal thing in the world to always sit behind his desk, leaning back in a comfortable chair, and start a conversation with his employees who are sitting on a straight, much smaller chair directly shapes his ideas about the relationship between manager and employees. The employee is, as it were, invited to play a role in his boss's 'script'. If he waits, impressed by the situation, the manager may think: 'No initiative among the employees here'. In doing so, he reaffirms his (script) belief: I told you so!

Reinforcement

The final reinforcement in such a situation is mainly derived from the behavior of the other person. The circle of the self-fulfilling prophecy is closing. The manager thought 'that it should mainly come from him in his department'. He therefore behaved as if the employee had nothing to say and should above all listen. And look: he was absolutely 'right'! Often we underline reinforcement with old memories of similar situations. Sometimes we seek out others to share aloud our view of ourselves, others, and the world/life. Bringing up the past often works out well.

The racket system is a closed circle, because we first believe something and then act on that belief, automatically having experiences that confirm our original beliefs. If we take this path often, deep ruts will naturally form, making it likely that we will take the same path in certain situations. That's more of the same and therefore not very effective! If you want a different outcome, you will have to do something else yourself. The good news is that the circle of any self-fulfilling prophecy can be broken in three places. A favorable turn can come from:

- the introduction of other, new beliefs;
- different, new behavior; and
- a different, new reaction to others.

New beliefs

Giving up a script belief is not easy. Beliefs do not stand alone. They are woven into a network of values and norms by which we live and work. Still, it can be wise to test certain beliefs by talking about them with others. Assume that your belief is just a hypothesis. Then look for verification or falsification. Be genuinely curious: (Peer) supervision – intervision is a very powerful tool here, which makes it possible to test beliefs and gain new ideas, thus breaking the circle. Read in this book about seven other ways to get things done (instead of the old idea of using power).

Actions

It is often easier to break the circle by showing different behavior. The manager in our example may decide to leave his desk and sit down with his employees. Or even better: to have a real meeting at the workplace. We mainly revise our beliefs when we have new experiences. This manager needs the concrete experience that his employees do have useful ideas and should experiment with seven other ways to get things done (instead of the old idea of using power).

Reinforcement

Those who want to gain a new experience without reinforcing old beliefs, for example, involve others early in ideas and plans for change. This way you can ask your employees in advance to respond 'as if our (!) change has already succeeded'. That can be a huge stimulus for the desired change. It is even sometimes claimed that for real change, you have to dare to start 'on the other side'. For behavioral change at management level, the reasoning goes, it is precisely the employees who should be trained to deal differently with the managers. Not entirely nonsense, we think.

Who is not strong must be smart?

As said, children are in a one-down position with respect to their parents, who are in a one-up position. The lessons learned in our early years are used by people in later life to 'stay in control' and thus maintain or improve their situation. Power games, says Steiner (1987).

In a workshop on power and management, the trainer asked a group of managers to write down a few thoughts in response to the question, 'How do you get your way if you really have to?' After everyone was open and honest, most of the participants were shocked and confused about the responses. The ease with which concepts such as 'coercion, threat, nag, intimidate, get angry, and punish' came to the table was worth more than a little self-examination to them.

Children learn from an early age that power equals being the boss. In many (script) beliefs, 'playing the boss' is the way to bring about change and get your way. In this way, according to Steiner, other ways of exerting influence are placed in a hierarchy (a ladder of success) in which it is 'boss above boss'. Such leaders naturally create followers and masters create slaves, creating a one-up/one-down chain in families, schools, churches, businesses, organizations, and countries. Steiner sympathizes with people who resist domination. Thinking in hierarchy often does not make use of a much broader spectrum of possibilities to bring about change and improvement. Using one or more of the seven alternatives presented in this book is a lot smarter than using power or force.

Will to power

One of the great thinkers about human behavior, Alfred Adler (1924), made the concept of power the core of his theory. He incorporated Nietzsche's 'will to power', as a driving force in human beings, into his individual psychology. He wondered how children seek opportunities to assert their power. Growing up in a world where almost everyone seems to be bigger and more powerful than themselves, the child looks for the easiest way to get what it needs. A 'split' in each child's life path ensures that they:

- either learn to imitate the adults in their environment in order to become more assertive (and powerful);
- or learn to 'consciously' show powerlessness in order to get help and attention in this way. The term 'inferiority complex' stems from Adler's thinking.

- Adler (1924) does distinguish four types, which clarify how a person has learned to deal with 'power':
  - the 'ruling types' strive for power over other people. They don't have to be nasty people at all. Many make great achievements. They like to make it clear to others that they are successful, sometimes in a less pleasant way. These are the dominant employees in organizations. In TA terms: winners script (Berne, 1972).
  - the 'receiving types' depend on other people. They are passive in life and often use manipulative behavior to 'force' what they need. These are the over-adjusted employees in organizations. In TA terms: losers script (Berne, 1972).
  - the 'avoiding types' try to get around problems. They want to avoid defeat. They are often seen as 'distant', and they often isolate themselves. These are the Einzelgängers in organizations. In TA terms: non-winners script (Berne, 1972).
  - the fourth, most healthy style we believe, is that of the 'socially engaged types'. They believe in doing good for the benefit of society and in their power over their own lives. Adler wrote about this:
    - This lifestyle must be practiced. This is only possible if one grows up in a sense of connection with others and feels part of a greater whole. One must become aware that not only the pleasant things in life belong to you, but also the unpleasant ones.
    - Being autonomous means being self-governing, determining one's own destiny, taking responsibility for one's own actions and feelings, and throwing off patterns that are irrelevant and inappropriate to living in the here-and-now.

Every individual strives for personal power, Adler believes, which is a form of personal identity. Central to his psychology is that people always strive for something. If this is done in a healthy way, the individual also adapts to its environment. In this way he can contribute to the greater good. The 'character', also a term of Adler, develops in the cooperation between these two opposing forces: the need for power (der Wille zur Macht) and the need for togetherness (Gemeinschaftsgefühl). Our scripted beliefs about power are based on 'the conclusions we made as children about how these forces worked for or against us'.

Talking about power: Nelson Mandela

We would like to close this first chapter with a quote from the former president of South Africa saying: 'The problem is not that I don't know how to use my power. Rather, the problem is that I don't know how not to use that power' (Kalungu-Banda, 2006). Those in power should keep this question on their minds and follow Mandela's trail more.

References

Adler, A. (1924) *The Practice and Theory of Individual Psychology*. London: Routledge.

Berne, E. (1961) *Transactional Analysis in Psychotherapy*. New York (NY): Grove Press.

Berne, E. (1972) *What Do You Say After You Say Hello?* London: Corgi Books.

Bradshaw, J. (1990) *Homecoming. Reclaiming and Championing Your Inner Child*. New York (NY): Bantam Books.

De Graaf, A. (2022) *Healing and Change: An Exploration of Options in the Therapy Room*, Transactional Analysis Journal, 51:3, pp. 267–275. www.tandfonline.com/doi/abs/10.1080/03621537.2021.1950364

De Graaf, A. and Kunst, K. (1998) *De Mythe van de Onschuldige Omstander (The Myth of the Innocent Bystander)*. Barneveld: Meso Magazine, 102, pp. 27–33.

Erskine, R. (1980) *Script Cure: Behavioral, Intrapsychic, and Physiological*, Transactional Analysis Journal, 10:2, pp. 102–106.

Erskine, R. and Zalcman, M. (1979) *The Racket System, a Model for Racket Analysis*, Transactional Analysis Journal, 9:1, pp. 51–59.

Foucault, M. (1966) *The Order of Things: An Archaeology of the Human Sciences*. London: Taylor & Francis.

Jacobs, A. (1987) *Autocratic Power*. Transactional Analysis Journal, 17:3, pp. 59–71. https://doi.org/10.1177/036215378701700303

Hay, J. (2009) *Working It Out at Work. Understanding Attitudes and Building Relationships*. Hertford: Sherwood Publishing.

Holdeman, Q. L. (1989) *The Symbiotic Chain*. Transactional Analysis Journal, 19:3, pp. 137–144. https://doi.org/10.1177/036215378901900304

Kalungu-Banda, M. (2006) *Leading Like Madiba: Lessons of Leadership from Nelson Mandela: Leadership Lessons from Nelson Mandela*. Lansdowne: Double Storey Books.

Karpman, S. (1971) *Options*, TAJ, 1:1. https://doi.org/10.1177/036215377100100115

Korda, M. (1991) *Power! How to Get It, How to Use It*. New York (NY): Grand Central Pub.

Ofman, D. (2001) *Core Qualities, A Gateway to Human Resources*. Schiedam: Uitgeverij Scriptum.

Robbins, T. (1995) Tony Robbins event in Brussels: Unleash the Power Within (UPW).

Steens, R. (1993) *Menselijke Communicatie (Human Communication)*. Antwerpen: Interaktie Akademie.

Steiner, C.M. (1987) *The Seven Sources of Power: An Alternative to Authority*, TAJ, 17:3. https://doi.org/10.1177/036215378701700309

Weiner, B. (1985) *An Attributional Theory of Achievement Motivation and Emotion*, Psychological Review, 92:4, pp. 548–573.

2   Grounded

A quirky view

A traveler met a shepherd on his way and asked him, 'What kind of weather will we have today?' The shepherd replied, 'The kind of weather I like'. The traveler asked, 'But how do you know it will be the weather you like?' The shepherd said, 'I've found, sir, that I can't always get what I like. I have therefore learned to like what I get. That's why I'm sure we'll get the weather I like today'.

A funny story with a powerful lesson. This shepherd has a strong view on something that is rather important to him. After all, a shepherd stays outside all day! He had his own quirky view on what the weather does that helps him (and his sheep) get through the days successfully. The power of a clear vision of what really matters is discussed later in this chapter. Eric Berne (1966) writes that being grounded is all about being well rooted in the here-and-now. He talks about an authentic human being as 'a human being well-grounded in the present and free of influences that do not pertain to the current moment' (p. 361). The power of the Adult ego state is indeed that it operates in the here-and-now and rationally processes what we are thinking and feeling, which is based on facts without interference of unconscious contamination.

Too much or too little

Steiner (1987) writes about managers who are grounded as managers who are well rooted and 'know what they stand for'. As a result, they stay stable and are not so quickly unbalanced. Neuropsychiatrist Dan Siegel (2012) describes life as a complex and self-managing system that seeks balance. It is precisely in this world that tends toward chaos that balanced leadership is essential. Those who are too firmly rooted in their own values and norms will become stubborn, hard,

DOI: 10.4324/9781003452386-2

and unattainable. Bob Pearson (1917–2008), an American general manager, believed that the greatest danger to his organization is 'rigidity'.

> The increasing demand for absolute answers to nitpicking questions, the pressure on our organization to enforce our traditions. Imposing more and more rules on employees and teams of employees. In this trend towards rigidity, we are drifting further and further away from what we as an organization can really be.

Those, on the other hand, who are insufficiently grounded will too easily blown with every wind direction. Before they know it, they always let someone else's opinion or thought prevail over their own. Employees no longer know where they stand with you. That insecurity can be devastating (https://aaagnostica.org/2012/03/07/aas-greatest-danger-rigidity/, accessed on April 19, 2023).

Sailing

For a management book, our previously published book *Einstein and the Art of Sailing* has, to say the least, a very unusual title. (Since the publication of the book in 2005, 60,000 copies have been sold. Since 2019, the book has been published under the title *Your Leadership Role and Professional Identity*.) It will soon become clear to most readers why the figure of Einstein is so central to the title. However, the metaphor of sailing is often not immediately clear. The book says about this:

> The art of sailing is that a sailor plays with two opposing forces. He makes use of the elements, letting the wind, the tides, and the current work for him. He also uses his own power to get the rudder and sail in the best position. His own power and the power of the elements are well matched at best. Managers also make use of their own personal strength, experience, knowledge, and skills. And they also know the possibilities and impossibilities of the system and the context in which they take up the role of manager. Excellent managers know both force fields, make adequate use of them and keep their organization on track.

This chapter is about how the manager stays on track. That requires power. What kind of power? Where do you get that from? Among many sources of power, the ability to be grounded is paramount for managers who want to achieve results.

Secure base leadership

Steiner is clear that being able to stand for something and especially daring (!) is a powerful source of influence. George Kohlrieser, professor of Leadership and Organizational Behavior, writes in his book *Hostage at the Table* (2006) that successful managers 'have several people around them to fall back on as an anchor in their lives'. Kohlrieser speaks of 'secure bases' here. The term 'secure base' comes from attachment theory. A secure base is an attachment figure, usually the primary caregiver, with whom a child has developed a secure attachment. This attachment figure serves as a base of security allowing the child to explore the environment with confidence. The child can count on the caretaker to welcome them on their return, comfort them if they are upset, and reassure them if they are scared. It doesn't take much imagination to replace 'parent' with 'manager' in the foregoing. Secure bases are mostly people but also goals and things with which we feel a special connection. They provide us with protection in the face of adversity, comfort when we feel defeated, and energy to face it again. For children – if everything goes well – the parents, grandparents, and/or educators often are a secure base. For adults, most secure bases are peer-related, that is, colleagues, friends, and family members. A base literally means: 'A structure or entity on which something draws or depends'. Not unimportant!

Often, there is also a special secure base group consisting of executives, coaches, trainers, and/or mentors – authority figures who have an important role or played a role in life and work. Kohlrieser is convinced that people are the happiest when they feel connected to someone who is there for them 'anytime of the day'. Knowing internally that the other is there is often enough. A secure base is an excellent starting point for every employee to sail new seas and make new discoveries. Without such a harbor it often becomes too big an adventure, and the sailor just keeps floating around at the first headwind.

To be able to stand for something – on good grounds – and specially to dare to stand for something, a number of secure bases are essential. Connection with people and connection with goals, Kohlrieser believes, contribute enormously to a solid self-image. In his book *Care to Dare* (2012), he states that every manager should know about three factors that make the difference:

- Trust: care, safety, reliability, fairness
- Clarity: direction, purpose, accountability, values
- Momentum: motivation, confidence, empowerment, connection

Those who are only connected to people (warmth) can feel safe but have little success. Those who are only connected to goals (adrenaline) can achieve considerable success but (inside) die of loneliness. Whoever has people as a secure base learns to love and be loved. This nurtures the sense of belonging and helps to stand up for the things that really matter. Whoever has goals as a secure base learns what it is to be competent. And that helps to tackle issues that really need to be addressed. The basis for an answer to the question 'What do you stand for?' starts at the beginning. With your answer to the question who and what your secures bases are.

The power of healthy attachment

Being grounded also refers to being well rooted and well connected. People who are well grounded are better able to calm down their emotions and stay centered. Healthy social and emotional development occurs when growing children have the opportunity to bond with at least one primary caretaker. Adrienne Lee (2008) puts it crystal clear when she writes: 'The process of attachment is about power and co-operation. . . . The child must give up on narcissistic control and replace it with something like co-operation (in order to keep "the other around")' (p. 37).

Anthony Sork (McTague, 2014) was one of the first to explore the concept of 'attachment' in its meaning for living and working in organizations. He shows that managers who treat their employees incorrectly during what he calls 'the critical attachment period' (about 120 days) have a bad influence on the degree of attachment that is achieved. The consequences for the organization are enormous. Think of a high dropout due to illness. Think of the risk of reduced commitment and performance. Think of a high turnover of employees. In the 120 days of the critical attachment period, it is about developing a sense of security, trust, acceptance, and belonging. In organizations in which the employees are well attached, an increased level of retention; performance; and contribution of new, existing, and transitioning employees is noticeable. After all, a healthy attachment is the basis for the ability to function independently and for the ability to enter into affective relationships.

It is natural to assume that healthy attached managers are better able to manage employees in such a way that they develop a sufficient level of attachment and commitment to have a fruitful time in the organization in which they work. Managers who are themselves insecurely attached and have difficulty with self-confidence will be less able to help their employees effectively through the critical attachment period.

Roots

The time when a motorist in an unfamiliar city had to seek refuge at an information column with a city map is long gone, but the way in which that happened is a nice illustration of what it means to know where you stand (and what you stand for). To find the route to the destination, you took two steps at the time. First you looked up the street where you needed to be in the alphabetical register and then found it via the index on the map. Then came the

most important thing: you looked for the arrow on the map that indicated =>
here you are. Without a clear arrow on the map showing your current position, the map would be worthless: you won't get anywhere if you don't know
where you are. So, if you want to get somewhere, it would be a good idea to
establish where you are standing! Being grounded has to do with the question of what you really want to stand for. What don't you step aside for?
What makes you say, 'Over my dead body'? Authentic and honest people
stand up for their cause and often make an indelible impression. Take a look
around your own organization and ask yourself which people you experience
as authentic and honest. What gives you that impression when you look at
their behavior and their way of communicating?

We feel the difference between a big mouth and really meant words.
When people use big words, 'values and norms' are often at stake. The Dutch
pedagogue Lea Dasberg (1975) became known for her groundbreaking book
Raising by Keeping Small. When asked what her orthodox Jewish upbringing
meant to her, she said,

> Fortunately, I was brought up with many certainties and guidelines. I say
> fortunately because I am convinced that every child, no matter how small,
> struggles with questions of conscience. What am I allowed to think, do
> and feel and what not? What is good and evil, naughty and sweet, beauti-
> ful and ugly? Educators need to provide clear answers to those questions.
> I got those answers.

Being grounded also concerns the fundamental role of values and norms in
the family, business, and society. It is certain that many young people today,
contrary to what Dasberg experienced, must collect their values and standards
from different sources. The postmodern climate of the past decades, in which
there is no single truth and in which many things are (or have become) rela-
tive, has left its mark. Pragmatism and opportunism seem to have become
the norm. Dasberg writes that her orthodox Jewish upbringing involved more
than offering 'certainties and guidelines'. She adds: 'I was brought up in a
culture of rituals and celebrations, which were decorated with things that a
child likes: nice clothes, good food and presents, the whole family together.
Those events enriched my life'. So it's not just about knowing what you stand
for as a manager. That is only the I-side of being grounded. But it is also about
the We-side: knowing in which tradition you are or want to be rooted. That
helps you to not be blown away at the first headwind or get off track too easily.

Moral leadership

In his book *De zin van zijn* (the sense of being), Maurice de Valk (2009)
invites his readers to record in their personal status, a rule of life, what is
really worthwhile for them. It is a reflection on one's personal philosophy,

constitution, a credo! De Valk offers the following questions (edited by us) to help discover one's personal status. This leads to questions such as: What is really important to me in my life and work? And why do I find that so important? What do I want to achieve with it, what am I aiming for, and who do I deeply want to be? What then is my mission in my life?

We ended Chapter 1 with a quote from Nelson Mandela. For many, he is a shining example of what moral leadership can do. For us, he is the example par excellence of a great, well-founded leader, showing in everything he did that one must never give up. Leaders should try to bring people together and be selfless. Following Mandela, it is clear to us that moral leadership refers to a leader's conduct that exemplifies strong moral values, selflessness, and integrity. Decision-making in moral leadership is guided by an inherent ethical system and moral purpose. Self-disciplined, compassionate, and responsible, moral leaders prefer to lead and inspire others by setting an example and establishing moral goals. Mandela's most famous quote, used during his inauguration speech in 1994, borrowed from Marianne Williamson (1992), is probably: 'Our deepest fear is not that we are inadequate. Our deepest fear is that we are powerful beyond measure. It is our light, not our darkness that most frightens us'. We learn here that it is not easy to stand for something and to stay there. It is not easy to live and work according to clearly chosen values and norms. Being and staying grounded, it is precisely with a headwind that frightens many. De Graaf (2022) writes that he experiences that many managers are (too) focused on managing their own fear and anxiety. Being powerful, having the right and the ability to make tough decisions (one of the manager's main tasks) makes many managers reluctant.

Kouwenhoven (2018) describes how what he calls an organizational Parent (ego state) system (OPS) can be used as an integrated steering system by which leaders can improve the effectiveness of their leadership style. This values-based leadership contributes to the development of a safe working environment, the well-being of employees, a positive reputation for the company, and a better world. Scary or not, managers will need to be grounded at key moments in their leadership careers. As a result (Steiner, 1987), they stay stable and are not so quickly unbalanced.

Grounded, rooted, and committed

The book *A Rule of Life for Beginners* by Wil Derkse (2021) is subtitled *Benedictine Spirituality for Everyday Life*. Due to our Calvinistic background, it took us a while before we took up this document from the Roman Catholic tradition. But to be fair: it turned out to be a gem! Derkse translates Benedictine life into forms of living together and working together outside the walls of the monastery: in everyday practice. The book is a source of zest for life and lifestyle, especially for those in a position of extra responsibility – especially for managers of whatever signature.

Benedictine spirituality is very down to earth and therefore fits in well with our theme of being grounded. Because under the Benedictine motto, anything worth doing is worth doing well, and the emphasis is on the ordinary things, even in spirituality. 'Spirituality', says Derkse, 'you can't bring it down. After all, it is meant for downstairs'. In Benedictine thinking, we remain beginners every day – but beginners on a pilgrimage to a better quality of life – and work, of course. The modern manager can be inspired by the monk, who remains a permanent apprentice, a beginner, attentively listening to what each new situation demands of him. This degree of being grounded, of commonplaceness, and of tranquility contributes to you not only being interested in people and the market, but also that you are actually committed to it. That really works a big step further!

Another point on which you can learn something from Benedict as a manager is the vow of *stabilitas*. It is translated as: don't run away from what you have committed yourself to and what appeals to you here-and-now, but stay with your community and don't run away too easily from the context for which you have been chosen. Every day offers countless opportunities to walk away but just as many opportunities to show commitment. This is how you become grounded, rooted, committed. And that matters, because what is not rooted does not endure and has no life force. We add to those wise words: . . . and therefore will not bear fruit.

A clear vision

The following quote from Andrew Carnegie (MacGregor, 2019), a Scottish-American industrialist and philanthropist, immediately makes clear what it means to stand for something: 'If you want to be happy, set a goal that commands your thoughts, liberates your energy, and inspires your hopes'. This 'man of steel' built up a sizeable industrial empire, partly because he stood for something. He knew what he wanted (among other things: happiness) and was grounded! Steiner's first words in the description of this source of power are that being rooted is about 'the capacity to stand one's ground'. A clear picture of the future, a compelling picture of where you want to go, a strong picture that others can lean on, is incredibly helpful. Our experience, as trainers, educators, and entrepreneurs, is that having a clear vision has at least three enormous advantages:

- Having a vision gives a sense of purpose and direction to yourself or the company. A good vision helps to define short- and long-term goals and contributes to making good quality decisions.
- If you work with others, or work in a company and a clear vision is defined, it supports the common good. This makes everyone feel like they are part of the bigger picture. This not only gives a deeper meaning to the work, but it also helps to bond in a team that is organized, focused, and works better together to jointly contribute to the vision and the result.

- A powerful vision is inspiring. It has a clear and motivating effect on yourself and everyone within the organization. It provides motivation, enthusiasm, energy; increases involvement; and stimulates change. This is especially important during difficult or stressful times, as having a clear vision will build willpower, discipline, and remind everyone why you do what you do. Think about the bigger picture.

Finally, we let Andrew Carnegie (2019) speak again: 'The world of great opportunity is available now, as it has always been, only for those with great vision'.

Talking about being grounded: Ellen Johnson Sirleaf

Former Liberian president (and Nobel laureate) Ellen Johnson Sirleaf has stood for human rights in general and women's rights in particular throughout her life. This is the belief that kept her grounded: 'Ethnicity should enrich us; it should make us a unique people in our diversity and not be used to divide us' (Johnson Sirleaf, 2010). Read more at: https://yourstory.com/herstory/2021/01/quotes-nobel-peace-laureate-ellen-johnson-sirleaf-liberia

References

Berne, E. (1966) *Principles of Group Treatment*. New York (NY): Grove Press.

Dasberg, L. (1975) *Grootbrengen door kleinhouden, als historisch verschijnsel* (Raising by Keeping Small, as a Historical Phenomenon). Meppel: Boom.

De Graaf, A. and Kunst, K. (2005) *Einstein en de Kunst van het Zeilen: Een Nieuwe Kijk op de Rol van de Leider*. Amsterdam: SWP Books.

De Graaf, A. and Kunst, K. (2010b) *Einsten and the Art of Sailing: A New Perspective on the Role of Leadership*. Hertford: Sherwood Publishing.

Derske, W. (2021) *Een Levensregel voor Beginners: Benedictijnse Spiritualiteit voor het Dagelijks Leven (A Rule of Life for Beginners: Benedictine Spirituality for Everyday Life)*. Tielt: Lannoo.

De Valk, M. (2009) *De Zin van Zijn, Voedsel voor de Ziel (The Meaning of Being, Food for the Soul)*. Delft: Meinema.

Johnson Sirleaf, E. (2010) *This Child Will Be Great: Memoir of a Remarkable Life by Africa's First Woman President*. New York (NY): Harper/Perennial.

Kohlrieser, G. (2006) *Hostage at the Table. How Leaders Can Overcome Conflict, Influence Others, and Raise Performance*. New York (NY): Jossey-Bass Inc.

Kohlrieser, G. (2012) *Care to Dare. Unleashing Astonishing Potential Through Secure Base Leadership*. New York (NY): Jossey-Bass Inc.

Kouwenhoven, M. (2018) *Values-Based Leadership and the Organizational Parent System*, Transactional Analysis Journal, 48:4, pp. 350–364. https://doi.org/10.1080/03621537.2018.1505131

Lee, A. (2008) *The Power Is in Our Process*, Transactional Analysis Journal, 38:1, pp. 36–42. https://doi.org/10.1177/036215370803800106

MacGregor, J. (2019) *Andrew Carnegie – Insight and Analysis into the Life of a True Entrepreneur, Industrialist, and Philanthropist*. Sheridan, WY: CAC Publishing LLC.

McTague, R. (2014) *Measuring Employee Attachment /Detachment in Human Resources*. In: Human Resources, October/November 2014.

Siegel, D. (2012) *The Whole-Brain Child. 12 Revolutionary Strategies to Nurture Your Child's Developing Mind*. New York (NY): Bantam Dell Pub Group.

Steiner, C.M. (1987) *The Seven Sources of Power: An Alternative to Authority*, TAJ, 17:3. https://doi.org/10.1177/036215378701700309

Van Poelje, S. and De Graaf, A. (2022) *New Theory and Practice of Transactional Analysis in Organizations: On the Edge (Innovations in Transactional Analysis: Theory and Practice)*. London: Routledge.

Williamson, M. (1992) *A Return to Love: Reflections on the Principles of "A Course in Miracles"*. San Francisco (CA): HarperOne.

3 Passion

Passionate painting

The story goes that Paul Cézanne selflessly painted masterpieces for 35 years. He just gave them away to his neighbors. He loved his job so much that he just didn't think about getting recognition and didn't spend time seeking it. It never occurred to him that he could ever be regarded as the founder of modern painting. He just wanted to paint. Passionate. He owed his first fame to a Parisian art dealer, who saw his paintings by accident and presented them to the art world in the first Cézanne exhibition. The world was stunned by his masterpieces. And the master himself was even more surprised. Leaning on his son's arm, he entered the exhibition room, and when he saw his own paintings hanging there, he turned to his son and couldn't say anything other than: 'Look, they framed them'.

Passion seems to be able to push other, sometimes quite important, matters into the background. It makes you forget time and space. Passion is a powerful resource to draw from that helps achieve goals. So-called success coaches shout in unison that you should mainly follow your passion. However, passion can also threaten your own well-being and that of others. Nevertheless, we choose to follow Steiner, who writes that passion is a hugely powerful source of influence. It is! It is passion that motivates the Natural Child ego state. Passionate people often get a lot done. Passion does not want to conquer but convinces by itself. It is heartwarming to meet a passionate person, someone who is on fire for a purpose in life. If someone can passionately tell a story, be it about collecting stamps or playing the triangle, you keep listening to them. What is the secret of passion?

Too little or too much

Claude Steiner (1987) says of passion:

> Nothing can give managers more influence than passion. It is the fire that moves and keeps them moving. The noticeable enthusiasm

DOI: 10.4324/9781003452386-3

for the high-quality product or service literally works accurately. Passion can be a wonderful gift, but if you're not careful, it can become an awful curse when there's little or too much.

Too little passion makes managers lifeless, dull, and cowardly. Bore-out (Crombach, 2021) is partly the result of not being in contact with what you are passionate about. If you're having a bore-out, it means you're stressed out because you're bored. You have little to do at work, you find the work boring, and you are not connected to what really matters to you. Poor employees. Too much passion makes them boil over with unbridled and often unfocused energy. Vallerand (2003) defines passion as a strong inclination toward an activity that people like, that they find important, and in which they invest time and energy. He writes that obsessive passion (OP) refers to a controlled internalization of an activity in one's identity that creates an internal pressure to engage in the activity that the person likes. Obsessive passion can do a lot of damage.

... with passion

You regularly come across the word 'passion' in job advertisements: 'Manager wanted with a passion for people' or 'Is building an effective team your passion? Then you are the team leader we are looking for!' or 'We expect a passion for healthcare from the new director'. But what is actually meant by passion here? What makes 'passion' such a powerful source of influence? Aren't the advertisements really just saying that they don't appreciate a nine-to-five mentality? Passion then seems no more than the reverse of passive. Or are these prospects looking for employees who are not satisfied with 'almost'?

Think back to your high school days: were you taught by a teacher who was full of his subject? A teacher who passionately explained 'the Pythagoras theorem' or enthusiastically talked about 'the peace of Versailles'? Who was that? How did that passion and enthusiasm manifest itself? What was the effect on you and your classmates? Even a transverse teenager can benefit from a teacher with passion. The ancient sage Confucius already understood that and said: 'Tell me and I will forget. Show me and I'll remember. Inspire me and I will get involved!' The power of passion.

The etymological roots of the concept of passion can, wonderfully enough, be found in the world of religion. That makes you think. If you look up the word 'passion' in an online dictionary, you will also read there: 'The suffering of Jesus'. After all, a passion is also a story, a play, a piece of music, or a visual work of art, which has the suffering of Jesus Christ as its point of departure.

The concept of 'passion' seems to connect Jesus and managers, certainly linguistically. That gets even more exciting when we say that 'passion' is almost synonymous with 'enthusiasm'. Passion is often seen as the superlative of enthusiasm. The word 'enthusiasm' comes from Greek and literally means 'the God (entheo) within (iasm)'. The etymology of the word points to its divine origin. And a manager with spirit? Enough . . . , back to passion. It is a word from the Greco-Roman world, mainly meaning 'suffering' or 'endurance'. It was not until many centuries later, from the sixteenth century, that the word is also used for someone who is full of enthusiasm.

Passion and perseverance

Leaving a high-flying job in consulting, Angela Lee Duckworth (2016) took a job teaching math to seventh graders in a New York public school. She quickly discovered that IQ wasn't the only thing separating the successful students from those who struggled. In her book, she explains her theory of 'grit' as a predictor of success. 'Grit' is defined as working strenuously toward challenges, maintaining effort and interest over years despite failure, adversity, and plateaus in progress.

Success in top sport often depends on the extent to which athletes are passionate about the sport they practice but at least also on the extent to which they have perseverance. The manager who combines the power of passion with the ability to overcome setbacks, to persevere, inspires his employees enormously.

Perseverance is the ability to achieve your goal despite setbacks. A go-getter does not give up easily and sticks to a certain idea or action. Perseverance is an important soft skill because it, especially in combination with passion, helps to achieve goals and achieve success. Perseverance certainly is a competence demanded by many professions. Mind you, that perseverance also has pitfalls such as not knowing when to stop or having too little trust in others.

Duckworth for instance shows in her book how teachers, working in some of the toughest schools, not only survive but also are able to inspire students. We are still in awe of the movie Dangerous Minds in which a teacher (played by Michelle Pfeiffer) uses her passion and perseverance to stimulate students from a disadvantaged situation to deliver an impressive tour de force.

Inspiration in organizations

Ofman's surprising book, called *Core Qualities: A Gateway to Human Resources* (2001), is 'a plea for the creative capacity in individuals and organizations'. It is about the creating human being in a creating organization. Added value arises when people and organizations behave as parts of a creative whole, pool their energy, and thereby achieve more. Highly desirable for organizations that want to deliver quality. Unfortunately, this too has fallen into the hands of the certification 'mafia'. ISO 9001 is the globally recognized standard in the field of quality management. The question is who really benefits here. Certification, in the sense of delivering quality, in that view is mainly 'doing everything according to the rules and procedures'. It seems to get in the way of what Ofman calls passion. Ofman provides an overview of the reasons customers give for leaving a supplier or service provider:

- one percent die or retire,
- three percent change jobs or city,
- five percent give orders to friends/acquaintances,
- nine percent try the competition,
- fourteen percent are dissatisfied with a product or service, and
- *sixty-eight percent change because of indifference at the supplier.*

Dropping out is therefore much less influenced by factors related to the product or service than by the (indifferent) attitude of the supplier or service provider. So, the question is how this indifference can make room for inspiration and passion. This question arises not only in all private companies but also in the public sector. There, the choice to change supplier or service provider is often considerably more difficult (think of healthcare and education) or sometimes very absent (government agencies). Service provision is an interactive process with the customer. The quality delivered is therefore strongly personal and hardly influenced by guidelines and rules. Ofman writes: 'Essentially, delivering quality is an expression of love. Love for your customer. Love for your colleagues. Love for work. The opposite of love is indifference. In an indifferent environment, the passion has disappeared. Wasn't it Beethoven who once exclaimed: 'A note played wrong can be excused. A note played without passion is unforgivable'?

In the heyday of thinking about quality in terms of quality control, Daniel Ofman wrote about, among other things, 'the drama of certified organizations'. Systems, with all their rules and guidelines, can become real passion killers. Quality is then no longer working with heart and soul on a product or service but ensuring that the rules and guidelines are observed. And that is the death knell for true inspiration.

Ofman distinguishes the **I**-side, the **We**-side, and the **It**-side of quality. The It-side represents the system, procedures, regulations, and structures. That is the domain of management techniques. This side has long been at the forefront of thinking about quality.

'It' is also the safest side. The outside! Rules are rules, functions can be described in a binding way, lists can be ticked off, procedures can be followed step-by-step, and KPIs can be counted. It is the favorite and comfortable domain of the manager who bases his behavior on the literal meaning of the word manager: *manu agere*! To avoid misunderstandings: the It-side is of eminent importance – facts matter, without figures results cannot be measured

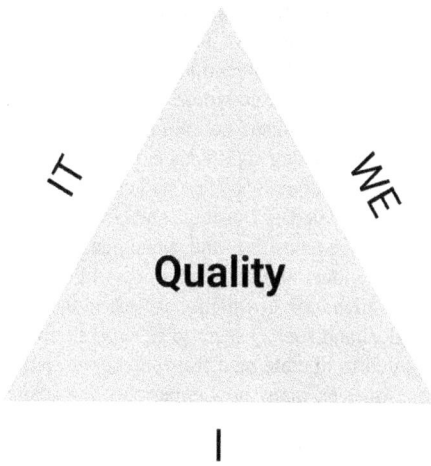

Figure 3.1 Quality is made of . . .

and of course nice plans and good procedures are extremely useful and so on. Without this data-driven information, passion degenerates into vague spirituality.

The We-side and I-side are less measurable, controllable, and manageable but mainly appeal to intuition and feeling. The We-side makes you think about questions such as: how does the current culture help or hinder successful progress, how is our cooperation experienced, how (inter)dependent are we on each other, which feelings play a role in this conflict or in this change, what kind of team are we, what is everyone's role and contribution at the moment, and what are the effects of our current team functions on our employees. Here, the emphasis is on that people have something to do with each other, with the intended goal and with the company they work for.

The I-side is about one's own passion, initiative, the will to deliver quality, and to take responsibility. The main question there is: What inspires me to deliver quality? This is the inside of quality. And that is decisive. It is the side of the uncertainty, the not yet knowing, the doubt, the unconscious – the inside. Passion has its own, nonquantifiable evidence. Without that passion, calculation degenerates into cold manipulation.

Amo ergo es!

Burger (2008) states that in our modern Western world, we are in a transitional phase between two eras. We seem to be approaching the end of the patriarchal, modern, and industrial yang era in which technology, competition, and hierarchy dominated and in which we thought the world was controllable and manageable. And at the same time, we are entering an era in which yin seems to be gaining ground, in which interaction and dialogue are becoming more central, and in which we see more and more examples of (international) cooperation based on equality and modern communication'. In a book about power, this is a statement of far-reaching significance. If Burger is right, the idea that power is mainly the control of many by few will come to an end. The new crop of young professionals, labeled by Boschma and Groen (2007) as the 'Generation Einstein' – a smart, fast, positive, and social generation – takes over.

Our society is the product of a constant process of ongoing individualization. The result is an alienation in which – at least in the perception of many people – the individual and society seem to be separate from each other. The Enlightenment wanted to liberate man from the oppressive structures of traditional societies. However, many now experience the adage of the Enlightenment – 'Cogito ergo sum' – as a too concise (and also incorrect) view of man. 'I think, therefore I am' has led to personal perspectives such as 'Just be yourself!' and 'I can decide for myself!' and to systemic perspectives such as 'Ultimately it is your own responsibility (and guilt)!' Both perspectives have driven individualization in the Western world. The adage of the new age could be: '*Amo ergo es*' – I love you, therefore you exist! Because of the one-sided emphasis on thinking (cogito), loving (amo) has been pushed to the sidelines. It's time to bring 'love and passion' back into the heart of the organization!

Power and sexuality

Passion and sexuality are closely linked. Passion is an important part of any satisfactory relationship. You could say that passion is the spark that keeps such a relationship going. Sexuality is part of passion. If you then consider that power can have the same effect as alcohol: it disinhibits people somewhat, and they get a certain narrowing of consciousness. The Parent ego state dissolves easily in alcohol, and examples of powerful people who behave (sexually) unethically abound. You only have to follow the news in recent years.

We are working on the final version of this chapter at a time when the football world has been turned upside down by the inappropriate sexual behavior of the President of the Spanish Football Federation. Power and sex lie close to each other if they are not already fully intertwined.

In that intoxicated state, powerful people take more and easier risks, especially in the sexual field. In combination with eroticized transference (Cornell et al., 2014), which can be seen as an intense, vivid, irrational erotic preoccupation with powerful people, characterized by often overt demands for love and sexual fulfillment, the employee's dependence on these powerful people runs a serious risk of ending up in unwanted and damaging situations. It is important for everyone to avoid such MeToo-like situations. People who can wield power in particular should take heed.

It is of the utmost importance to recognize transgressive behavior. Don't be naive about the connection between power and sexual misconduct. The media are often filled with reports of sexual misbehavior of those who were in charge in recent years. Anyone who understands anything about erotic transference will mainly address the powerful perpetrators of their inappropriate behavior.

Talking about passion: Barack Obama

Former US President Barack Obama was a huge fan of 'passion' as a source of power.
In an interview he said:

I think that at a certain stage those early ambitions burn away, partly because you achieve something, you get something done, you get some notoriety. And then the particularities of who you are and what your deepest commitments are beginning expressing themselves. You're not just chasing the idea of 'me' being important, but you, rather, are chasing a particular passion.

(November 2016, *Barack Obama and Doris Kearns Goodwin: The Ultimate Exit Interview*; www.vanityfair.com)

References

Berne, E. (1972) *What Do You Do After You Say Hello? The Psychology of Human Destiny*. Ealing (UK): Corgi Books.

Boschma, J. and Groen, I. (2007) *Generatie Einstein, Slimmer, Sneller en Volwassener (Generation Einstein, Smarter, Faster and More Mature)*. Utrecht: A.W. Bruna Uitgevers.

Burger, Y. (2008) *Menselijkheid in Organisaties (Humanity in Organizations)*. Amsterdam: Vrije Universiteit.

Cornell et al. (2014) *Into TA, a Comprehensive Textbook on Transactional Analysis*. London: Karnac.

Crombach, M. (2021) *Bore-Out, Een Praktische Handleiding voor Begeleiders (Bore-out, A Practical Guide for Facilitators)*. Delft: Eburon.

Duckworth, A. (2016) *Grit: The Power of Passion and Perseverance*. New York (NY): Simon & Schuster.

Offman, D. (2001) *Core Qualities, a Gateway to Human Resources*. Schiedam: Scriptum Uitgeverij.

Steiner, C.M. (1987) *The Seven Sources of Power: An Alternative to Authority*, TAJ, 17:3. https://doi.org/10.1177/036215378701700309

Vallerand, R., Blanchard, C., Mageau, G., Koestner R., Ratelle, C., Léonard, M., and Gagné, M. (2003) *Les Passions de l'Âme: On Obsessive and Harmonious Passion. (The Passions of the Soul: On Obsessive and Harmonious Passion)*, Journal of Personality and Social Psychology, 85:4, pp. 756–767.

4 Empathy

What's love got to do with it?

A little boy went to play in the neighbor's garden. The neighbor's wife had recently died, and now the old man was all alone. The boy saw that he was crying on his garden bench. He climbed onto the neighbor's lap and sat there very long and very still. Later, his mother asked what he had said to the distressed neighbor. 'I did not say anything. I just helped him cry'.

Much has been said, and much more can be said about 'love'. Almost every pop song has love as its theme. Almost everyone has heard Jennifer Rush's hit song: The power of love. The boy in the story above knows what it is. Yet, it is far from self-evident to use love in relation to management. Steiner (1987), however, seems to consciously choose to put love as a source of power at the heart of his article. We choose to take empathy as a starting point. Empathy is an important part of a loving relationship. However, it is more than or slightly different from love. Empathy helps the other person feel understood. It raises the question: How does it look from their perspective? After all, empathy is the ability to understand the other person's feelings. That demands something from the manager. We adhere closely to Steiner's ideas about 'a stroke-centered TA' (Steiner, 2003). A healthy exchange of strokes has a major influence on our thinking about what really matters to organizations.

Too little or too much

If the power of empathy is underdeveloped, a person is cold, incapable of experiencing own and other's feelings or benefiting of strokes from self or others, unable to nurture or to be nurtured. As a result, employees feel neglected. In this chapter, we will consider in detail the concept of 'the neglected organization' (Emrys Lamé, 2008). How do you recognize neglect, which interventions do work in such a situation, and

DOI: 10.4324/9781003452386-4

what is needed for recovery? A neglected organization is an organization that, due to a lack of true empathy for the employees, has not been guided and directed in its development. This leads to a developmental delay, as pedagogy teaches us.

When this form of power is overdeveloped or fixated, people feel driven to excessive sacrifices and of giving themselves away to others while neglecting themselves. The result is that employees behave dependently. All kinds of victim and rescuer-driven games (Berne, 1964) are the result, with all the detrimental consequences for relationships in the workplace. Playing games can be seen as a form of experience theft. It is precisely this experience that is so necessary for personal development.

Both too much and too little empathy can lead to the experience of being neglected. Managers can exploit the power of empathy. Empathy also has the ability to bind people and enables people to realize what initially seemed hardly impossible.

Evolutionary achievement

In his book *The Age of Empathy* (2009): *Nature's Lessons for a Kinder Society*, Frans de Waal emphasizes the importance of empathy for the humankind. Empathy is part of our evolution, an ancient innate ability selected over time, whose survival value has been tested again and again. Evolution has endowed us with a tendency to feel for others. Why? Simply because it benefited the average ancestor in the long run.

Relying on an automatic sensitivity to faces, bodies, and voices, humans have known empathy from the very beginning. Throughout the 200-million-year evolution of mammals, females with compassion for their offspring had greater reproductive success than cold, aloof mothers.

In Romanian orphanages, during the dictator Ceaușescu's time, we saw what happens when children are exposed to an emotional gulag. A nightmare without any human warmth produced children who could neither cry nor laugh, who could not play, and often spent the day in the fetal position.

So, empathy is not a deliberate decision that requires assuming a role, higher cognitive abilities, or even language. Identification and emotional involvement suffice. Even though it is obviously incorporated in us, you can tone down or strengthen the tendency of empathy. Relativization or even denial is possible. Without compassion and ethical standards, managers become snakes in suits, thriving in an economic system that also rewards such behavior.

Evolution rarely throws anything away, notes De Waal. Structures are transformed, changed, annexed for other functions, but always the old remains present in the new. The most powerful support for the common good comes from enlightened self-interest: from the realization that we are ultimately better off if we work together!

Is there a relationship between power and empathy in leadership? Power is about being goal-oriented, acting, performing, and getting results. Empathy is about being relationship-oriented, listening, connecting, trusting, and showing loyalty. Empathy is a form of emotional intelligence that enables the manager to gain insight into what is going on inside the other person. A good leader can dance between power and empathy, depending on the situation and the people. A leader who only uses power loses his team. A leader who uses only empathy loses his direction. A leader who combines power and empathy wins both respect and commitment.

Adrenaline and warmth?

In his article 'Team leadership and coaching', De Jong (1995) emphasizes the importance of the manager's monitoring of the balance between the 'hard' and 'soft' side for the success of the team. Two things should always be kept in mind by the manager:

- Adrenaline: the fuel needed to perform – the drive that propels the team forward
- Warmth: the climate in which people are willing to do things for each other, to cooperate

It is wise for every manager to regularly ask the question how the adrenaline in my team is on a scale of 1 to 10 and the warmth also on a scale from 1 to 10. Are both aspects sufficiently present? Are both aspects to create a successful team well balanced? What to do if the balance tips one way or the other? With these two concepts, we can distinguish between four types of teams that are given as follows.

Type 1: team Les Misérables (no adrenaline, no warmth)

Without adrenaline and without warmth, of course, nothing will happen with this team. There is no bond to each other and no bond to a result to be achieved. Everyone goes their own way but in which direction is not clear. It's still called a team, but it's actually just a collection of individuals. The whole is less than the sum of its parts. And what can be said about leadership? The manager failed to create sufficient urgency and sufficient connection. Time to say goodbye?

Conclusion for the team: demoted or even abolished, but at least a very strong intervention from the outside is needed.

Type 2: team Lean and Mean (more adrenaline than warmth)

In this team, only performance counts. The players act like mercenaries for whom performance is paramount. If conflict is necessary, it is certainly not avoided. Everything revolves around the intended result. Those who cannot join for whatever reason, who don't want to join, who don't dare to join, they are outside the team. If someone falls victim to the ever-increasing pressure, it is inherent to the system, and at best it is a pity. The deadline is approaching. The team is 'cool' and task-oriented, and as long as you are part of it, it feels like the perfect kick. But with regard to the relationship orientation, the mutual connection, and attachment, things are poor. The manager calculates very hard on the individual contribution, the personal scores, and targets. Nevertheless, it is a team with potential: sparks fly, and no effort is too much. If the manager succeeds in increasing the functional warmth, cohesion, and bonding, the perspective of this team will grow. And it goes without saying that the manager sets a good example: leadership is showing the way by going first!

Conclusion for this team: a project team that has only a limited lifespan can sometimes afford to sail mainly on adrenaline and little warmth.

Type 3: team Country Club (more warmth than adrenaline)

Everything in this team revolves around atmosphere, togetherness, and conviviality. It feels like a warm bath. You soon feel at home. On a personal level, they have a lot in common. People do not judge each other on results (which are often unnamed or at least diffuse). Conflicts are avoided, and there is always an excuse why goals (if any) are not achieved. If the atmosphere remains good, nobody has to fall by the wayside. Yet, this team is also a team with potential. After all, attention is paid to every fellow player, there are no big egos in the way, people are willing to work together, and there is a promising working climate. The manager who has an eye for what is missing, namely sufficient adrenaline, and who is able to invest in it can eventually reap the fruits of his efforts. The manager invests in development and training: individually and as a team. Finally, discipline will become normal behavior that will be demanded and demanded from all team members.

Conclusion for this team: a starting team works best together in an atmosphere of safety and trust. However, there must come a time when adrenaline is added – first commitment, then discipline.

Type 4: Dream team (balance between adrenaline and warmth)

In the Dream team, you will find the right amount and balance of adrenaline and warmth. There is plenty of bonding to each other, but people feel equally committed to the intended result. The goals are clear and shared by everyone. Deadlines matter! That challenge gives the team the energy to perform together, with everyone's part being different and being valued. The leadership excels through a healthy balance between support (warmth) and control (adrenaline). The leader shows authentic behavior and is autonomous, he uses the knowledge and experience of his players/employees, and his style is facilitating and coaching. As you take concrete steps in the desired direction, take occasional time outs to evaluate. Do so on your own, with your staff and with the team. Is the whole already more than the sum of its parts? If there is reason to, make sure there is something to celebrate regularly!

Conclusion for this team: the Dream team has everything it takes to be successful and to become a champion!

If as a manager, you look back at the teams you were part of, can you determine in retrospect which category the teams fall into? Have you ever been part of 'Les Misérables'? How did that turn out? What was your share? What did you do that you think in hindsight was not smart? What did you not do, that in retrospect, you think you should have done?

Empathy, strokes, and health

Research (https://uthealthaustin.org/blog/health-benefits-of-empathy, accessed on May 21, 2023) shows that empathy mainly leads to better health. People who feel understood experience the benefits of empathy such as:

- a longer life,
- less sadness,
- lower blood pressure,
- less anxiety,
- less stress,
- less suffering from acute pain, and
- faster recovery from illness.

In his book *Games People Play* (1963), Berne laid out stroke theory and made it clear that he considered strokes to be the fundamental motive for human behavior and the reason why people play games. People need strokes to survive physically and psychologically. From Claude Steiner's article on Stroke-Centered Transactional Analysis (p. 178): 'Strokes are transactional units of recognition. Wide-ranging research (Field, 2002; Omish, 1999) has shown that strokes are required for actual survival in young children and psychological survival and health in grown-ups'.

He or she must remain actively engaged with the client in pursuing a clear contractual goal and in using the group environment to further that process. Although TA in the early days mainly focused on improving (group) therapy practice, many insights and approaches are perfectly applicable to the daily practice of the manager. Managers must remain actively engaged with their employees in pursuing a clear contractual goal and in using the organizational environment to further that process. For all of them, it is a challenge to practice empathy, attunement, and kindness while avoiding codependency or rescuing.

After all, playing games mainly produces negative strokes. Those negative strokes then mainly confirm all kinds of scripted beliefs on the part of the manager and on the side of the employees.

The proximity effect

In social psychology, the proximity principle suggests that people closer together in a physical environment are more likely to form a relationship than those farther away. This paragraph invites you to examine your capacity for empathy. It reflects the question of how close you can be and how far you sometimes are from your employees. The closeness created by empathy leads to a soulful meeting: a real meeting with a living soul!

One of the reasons why proximity matters to attraction is that it breeds familiarity; people are more attracted to that which is familiar. Just being around someone or being repeatedly exposed to them increases the likelihood that we will be attracted to them.

Grafting

Empathy is derived from the Greek word 'em-patheia'. Literally it means 'in feeling'. Empathy is the ability to empathize with another. You empathize with someone and put yourself in his or her perspective. It is a special form of emotional intelligence. If you have a good understanding of what occupies people and what moves them, you can manage them much more effectively. What you have done is a communicative 'pacing'. Pacing is a first and necessary condition to be able to 'lead'. Many managers mainly want to lead. After all, you're a manager, aren't you? And managers have good, even better, ideas. They also have good, even better, opinions. They know very well, even much better than others, which way to go. They know well, even better, what is good for another. And they want to convince the other person of that – the faster the better. And if it is not possible, then by force or coercion. It doesn't work that way! This one-up approach usually leads to unwanted effects among employees. Possible effects are:

- the other person does not feel taken seriously;
- the other mainly experiences criticism;
- the other feels belittled;
- the other flees into adapted behavior;

- the awareness of the usefulness of their own efforts diminishes;
- the sense of having a say in how things are done ebbs away; and
- cooperation will be (even) more difficult in the future.

If you want to exert influence without power, it is wise to join in first. To ask yourself what inspires and preoccupies the other person, what his view of reality is. That requires (sincere) real interest, being able to listen carefully and take note of the 'other side'. That other side has an inside that you can't easily access. Some other people don't dare to show their insides so easily. Asking questions and listening help you access it.

An image we like to use to clarify the meaning of empathy is grafting. Grafting is a term used in fruit and tree cultivation and refers to the uniting of two plants to form a new plant. Part of a plant, the graft, is attached to another plant, the rootstock. In this way, the new is united with the existing. The fact that a small wound occurs at the attachment indicates that such a process cannot be completely painless. But the result may be there! Grafted trees and shrubs appear to bear fruit faster (and more).

Respect!

Empathy and respect are of course two different things, but they are deeply connected. In an empathic relationship, respect is an important part. Respect ensures that you accept each other as you are and that you give each other space for further development. Respect thus seems to be an important condition for successful cooperation. Respect is a word that is used in many ways and in many tones in our modern times. It seems like everyone is talking about the same thing, but the reality often is completely different. Apparently, respect has become one of those container-words into which everyone throws their own meaning. You must respect! But what should you actually do?

The Flemish clinical psychologist Flor Peeters (College notes, 2004) attempted to better understand this meta-concept, to concretize it, and to make it usable for everyday practice. After all, it is ultimately about converting respect, which is no more than a notion, into visible behavior. And behavior is communication and vice versa: communication is behavior. Peeters divided the concept of respect into the following behaviors, with which you can practice respect:

- Dwell on experiences

In conversations, it is important to keep realizing that both interlocutors speak from different experiences. In groups, it is even more complex. In the event of differences, there is a great temptation to quickly skip careful imaging and express opinions. A wise guru did it differently. When he was interrupted rather sharply and critically by an attendee during a meeting, he asked the question: 'What's your experience?' That took the sting out of the anger and started the real conversation.

• Hearing good intentions

The meaning of your communication lies in the effect you evoke. Sometimes that effect is not beneficial, while your intentions were so good. Conversely, this also applies to the other. If you can ignore the (negative) effects of the other person's words on you for a moment and, above all, continue to see the good intention behind those words, your conversation will take a turn for the better.

• Have an eye for feelings

In organizations, people sometimes pretend that emotions don't exist. Have you ever experienced a meeting full of repressed but palpable emotion? One of those meetings where everyone pretended nothing had happened: 'We'll quickly move on to the next item on the agenda . . . .'

• Taking up meanings

Every person is a unique signifier. That sometimes makes it so darn difficult to understand each other properly. My meanings are not yours. Therefore, be a real Einstein and especially ask what the other person thinks is the meaning of what he says or intends.

• Hearing change wishes

We sometimes wish things were very different. But the words we use are sometimes horribly inadequate, and our emotions often run away with us. How lucky to have a manager who doesn't immediately feel personally attacked or hurt! And what bad luck if you find a manager who cannot tolerate criticism of the organization. What a privilege if you have a manager who can see behind those difficult words and emotional expressions the sincere commitment and the deep desire to do things differently and better.

Those are some ideas that make it more possible to practice respect literally!

The neglected organization

In recent years, more and more attention has been paid to the question of how gamy patterns in organizations hinder managers and their employees in the optimal realization of organizational objectives or business results. It is clear that a nonoptimal stroke climate can lead to a great tendency to play games in order to meet their own stroke needs. In research into ineffective patterns in organizations (Emrys Lamé, 2008), the orthopedagogical metaphor is used. Just like parents who help their child to develop into an autonomous adult by being caring, accessible, and responsive, managers do this – if all goes well – in the relationship with their employees. In neglected organizations, defined as organizations in which the physical, emotional, normative, and educational needs of employees are not met (Van Hekken, 1992), employees appear to behave like neglected children. The dynamics in such an organization have a high level of game, such as the dynamics around a neglected child, its parents, and the wider environment. Neglect is sometimes caused and always followed by a dysfunctional manager–employee relationship with lots of game and few real encounters.

The Australian organizational consultant Anthony Sork (2007) works with the hypothesis of the 'critical attachment period'. Employees who, after 120 days, still do not experience the context in which they work as a place where they are accepted for who they are, as a place that is reliable and safe, and as a place where they have the experience of belonging are not going to give the best they have. Underperformance and absenteeism are becoming the norm. To be able to explore, experiment, and innovate in the workplace, people need a secure attachment.

Life is a paradox

'Shall we merge?', the chicken suggests to the pig. 'Bacon and eggs seem to me to be a world product'. The pig says after some thought: 'Wait a minute, you lay the eggs, but I'm going to die'. 'Yes . . . And? That's how it always goes with mergers', says the chicken.

Empathy is also the art of connecting. The metaphor of grafting makes this very clear. After grafting, the graft is tied by the horticulturist with grafting tape or raffia. The wound is then treated with grafting wax. That requires respectful attention. The manager who wants to deal with power differently tries to connect the thinking of the other person with his own thinking. That is vulnerable, but if it succeeds, the multiplication is fruitful and sustainable: from the old and new thinking, a completely new thinking arises, which does full justice to both, a kind of co-creation. That effort is fruitful, but it is certainly not completely painless. However, it is not possible without pain. For pain you can also read: loss. That goes for any change. Changes usually do not come about because people do not dare to face the pain – the loss – in the short term and are 'ignorant' about the possible profit in the future.

There is something strange going on with how people 'connect', it seems. Bion (1961) believed that there is an innate need for people to be in a community or group and to belong and a constant conflict with that need and our fear of annihilation and the need to be an individual. Bion saw that humans are group animals at war with their groupishness.

Each of us has a need to fit in and a need to be alone, a need for togetherness, and a need for apartness, a need for integration and one for differentiation.

We like to say 'we', but we also want to be able to say 'I'. Empathy that creates too much closeness can count on a response to prefer to keep some distance. The empathy of the other side can even disappear completely for a while. Where you say too much 'we' in your team, the 'I' will sound more and more. Team building is good, but know that no one trades individuality for the team. There is a time to work together and a time to do it alone. A solid wave of mergers is usually followed by a disentanglement in order to regain individuality.

Those who allow Bion's perhaps somewhat strongly accentuated words to get through need not be surprised or confused by this. Bion would probably say that it's just the way it is! The dynamics of empathy can be summarized as follows: where integration is a fact, differentiation becomes (by itself!) a need, and where differentiation is a fact, integration (by itself!) becomes a need. That always hurts a little because it always means a little loss. Anyone who then has sufficient empathy can handle this limit of empathy well. Life is a paradox!

Talking about empathy: Jacinda Ardern

New Zealand's former Prime Minister Jacinda Ardern stole many hearts by the loving way she led the country:

> I really rebel against this idea that politics has to be a place full of ego and where you're constantly focused on scoring hits against each one another. Yes, we need a robust democracy, but you can be strong, and you can be kind.
>
> (Jacinda Ardern on NBC's Today Show, September 25, 2018, interviewed by hosts Hoda Kotb and Savannah Guthrie)

References

Berne, E. (1968) *Games People Play*. New York (NY): Grove Press.

Bion, W. (1961) *Experiences in Groups and Other Papers*. London: Tavistock Publications.

De Jong, W.J. (1995) *Teamleiderschap en coaching (Team Leadership and Coaching)*, Leidinggeven en organiseren, 45.

De Waal, F. (2009) *The Age of Empathy: Nature's Lessons for a Kinder Society*. London: Souvenir Press.

EmrysLamé, M. (2008) *Verwaarloosde organisaties. Een onderzoek naar hechtingsstijlen tussen medewerkers en leidinggevenden. (Neglected Organizations. A Study of Attachment Styles between Employees and Managers)*. Utrecht: Faculteit Sociale Wetenschappen, Psychologie, Universiteit Utrecht.

Field, T. (2002) *Massage therapy*. Complementary and Alternative Medicine, 86, pp. 163–171.

Omish, D. (1999) *Love and survival*. New York (NY): Harper Collins.

Peeters, F. (2004) Notes for a Course at the Interaktie Akademie in Antwerp: Leiding geven, methodische werkbegeleiding (Leadership, Methodical Work Guidance). Antwerp: Interaktie Akademie.

Simson, N. (2007) *Attachment before engagement.* Naomi's BLOG: https://www.shcbond.com/wp-content/uploads/2014/10/Attachment-Before-Engagement-Nov-2007.pdf

Steiner, C. (2003) *Core Concepts of a Stroke-Centered Transactional Analysis,* Transactional Analysis Journal, 33:2, April 2003, pp. 178–181. https://doi.org/10.1177/036215370303300209

Steiner, C.M. (1987) *The Seven Sources of Power: An Alternative to Authority,* TAJ, 17:3. https://doi.org/10.1177/036215378701700309

van Hekken, S.M.J. (1992) *'Verwaarlozing: Achtergronden, Gevolgen en Behandeling'.* In: H. Baartman en A. Van Montfoort (red.), *Kindermishandeling: resultaten van multidisciplinair onderzoek ('Neglect: Backgrounds, Consequences and Treatment'.* In: H. Baartman and A. Van Montfoort (ed.), *Child Abuse: Results of Multidisciplinary Research).* Utrecht: Data Medica, pp. 166–185.

5   Control

Here-and-now

Someone who had meditated a lot in his life was once asked why he could always be so calm and controlled despite his busy work. He replied, 'If I stand, I stand. If I go, I go. As I sit, I sit. If I eat, I eat. If I speak, I speak'. Then the questioners caught him off guard and said, 'Surely we do that. But what do you do that goes above and beyond that? He said again, 'If I stand, I stand. If I go, I go. As I sit, I sit. If I eat, I eat. If I speak, I speak'. And again, the others said, 'We do the same! However, he said to them, 'No! If you sit, you are already standing. If you stand, you are already going. And if you go, you are already arriving at your destination'.

Self-control can be defined as the conscious control of incoming impulses. A Zen teacher (personal communication, February 2006) once asked us: 'If you're walking on the beach and your mind is all about the meeting you just left or the conversation you're about to have, have you been to the beach?' Good question with an obvious answer. Impulses to leave the here-and-now can really be anything and come from both external and internal. Everything you see, hear, smell, taste, or feel.

Self-control is only possible with focus and full awareness. Impulse control takes place in the prefrontal cortex. This part of the brain is involved in making more conscious choices about what to do or not to do. More about self-control and the brain will come later. Self-control is important, so that you stay in control and don't let your emotions or urges lead you rashly.

Too much, too little

Claude Steiner (1987) says of self-control:

> Control (over one's own emotions) gives managers power over themselves in the form of self-discipline. This allows them to

DOI: 10.4324/9781003452386-5

regulate their own sources of influence. This is crucial when things become difficult and complex around them. Those with too little controlling power soon become victims of their own inner confusion and, in its wake, of the outside world.

A lack of self-control can have many undesirable effects – disinhibition, excess, extravagance, and more. Managers without self-control will fall short, especially in times when things become difficult and complex. The Adult ego state, where we think, listen, and collect data according to the reality in the here-and-now, cannot be missed! Too much self-control can lead to a lack of spontaneity and creativity. Excessive self-control can even lead to cardiovascular diseases and depression with the manager. Emotion is motion! Those managers who want to get things moving will have to find the necessary fuel in their reservoir of emotions. Well thought-out please!

Managers are expected to act. It is important that they ensure that their actions are based on well-considered decisiveness.

It is not good for people to be carried away by their thoughts or feelings. This is at the expense of their autonomy. The most important skill for any human being is to learn to create a moment of reflection between impulse and action. This is self-control!

Empath and psychopath

The first book on emotional intelligence was by Daniel Goleman (1996). He begins with these words from the Greek philosopher Aristotle: 'Anyone can become angry; it is not difficult. But to get angry at the right person, in the right degree, at the right time, with the right intention and in the right way, that's not easy'. That is why it is very important to deal with emotions in a smart way. For emotionally literate managers, they can do a lot of good.

In 1997, Claude Steiner published a wonderful book entitled *Emotional Literacy: Intelligence with a Heart*. Self-control, a form of exerting influence, is one of the themes he discusses in this book. This paragraph is our interpretation and representation of some of the thinking in that book. Power in the world, the author suggests with a big wink, seems to be in the hands of two types of people: psychopaths, who feel nothing, and empaths, who are deeply in touch with the feelings of others. At one end of the spectrum, the psychopaths seem to live without the hindrances of other mortals. They can lie, steal, extort, maim, and kill without feeling guilty. When they gain influence over others, they can become extremely powerful. They are everywhere: not only in (world) politics but also in business. At the other end of the spectrum, empaths owe their power mainly to their emotional skills. They seem to possess an innate empathy. Their talent is to get the best out of people, and this sometimes gives them enormous opportunities to influence those around them. They are often very powerful in their own way.

Of course, these are extremes, which we're sure you can also recognize in yourself. Some will lean more toward one end of the spectrum and others more toward the other. Sometimes you may react with insensitivity or bluntness, and other times you will be full of sympathy for someone else. Many people with power are of course neither completely psychopathic nor entirely empathetic but move somewhere between the two extremes.

Where you place yourself on this polarity affects your ability to deal with difficult emotional situations – situations that lead to anger, sadness, fighting, fleeing, lying, lashing out at others, and hurting them. Psychopaths probably miss the charge and accompanying message entirely. Thus, an opportunity to do the right thing is lost. Empaths, before they realize it, get completely carried away by the situation and lose the ability to exert beneficial influence. The old advice to count to ten before reacting is therefore not so crazy. This applies even more so when (highly charged) emotions are involved. Those who are able to control themselves and keep thinking can exert more favorable influence than those who allow themselves to be led by numbness or hypersensitivity.

Anger management

In recent years, there has been much ado in the media about managers (and other leaders) who time and again cross the boundaries of decency. They explode in anger, slam doors, and threaten dismissal and more misery. Anger can sometimes seem like a monster. Something that can pop up at any moment and have terrible consequences. You say things you don't want to say, you destroy things, and you may even be physically aggressive toward others. Apparently, the pressure in many companies and organizations is so high that 'managers and employees boil over'. Because the prevailing culture and the existing structure cannot be easily changed, following a substantial anger management lesson seems to be a good choice for many of them.

When some people get angry, they lose control completely. They feel that the anger completely overwhelms them. But why is this happening? Tantrums can have various causes. Not infrequently, upon further investigation, the cause is found in trauma during childhood or adolescence. The script that results from such traumatizing experiences ensures that the autonomous way of dealing with anger is not addressed.

Steiner's book on achieving emotional literacy (1996) shows individuals how to open their hearts and minds to honest and effective communication, how to survey the emotional landscape, and ultimately how to take responsibility for their emotional lives. He states that emotional skill means going through three stages:

1. opening your heart,
2. exploring the emotional landscape, and
3. taking responsibility.

Opening your heart is the first step because the heart is the symbolic seat of our emotions. Good feelings, such as being happy, joyful, or in love, and bad feelings, such as being angry, sad, or afraid, reside in our hearts. Folk wisdom has known for centuries what neurology is learning to understand more and more intrusively in our days. I have a broken heart! (I have intense sadness). My heart leaps up! (Of joy). My heart turns over in my body! (I am disgusted). I hold my heart tight! (I am very worried). Dutch has more than 60 folk sayings with the word heart in them. English has even more – break someone's heart, cross your heart and hope to die, eat your heart out, follow your heart, from the bottom of my heart, get at the heart of the matter, be halfhearted about something, have a change of heart, and much more.

Exploring the emotional landscape is step 2. This is about taking emotions seriously by exploring, acknowledging, and sharing them. Old wounds are recognized and acknowledged as old wounds, so that the integration of humiliations and misconceptions can take place – a process of becoming whole. The need to act them out in the here-and-now decreases.

Steps 1 and 2 help managers, as step 3, to take more and more responsibility for the role that emotions play in their work. Those who are emotionally skilled deal with people more easily, know how to value everyone, and experience an increased sense of self-worth. Emotionally adept managers understand or hear their own emotions, know how to listen, and are able to express feelings honestly and convincingly.

The little brain

In neurology, the term 'the little (or other) brain', when it comes to the heart, is gaining currency (Armour, 2007). Opening your heart has everything to do with what is the theory about strokes in TA. The 'stroke myths', an invention of Steiner, are a set of rules imposed on us by our own negative Critical (cultural) Parent, the critical voice we carry with us that prevents us from giving and accepting strokes. In such a (work) climate, it is difficult to open your heart. The rules that our negatively Critical (cultural) Parent would like to impose on us are the following:

- Don't give the strokes you want to give.
- Don't ask for the strokes you desire.
- Don't accept the strokes you look forward to.

- Don't refuse the strokes you do not want.
- Don't give yourself strokes if you feel like it.

When the initial work is done and you have opened your heart, you can look at the emotional landscape you are in. You can learn what you feel: are you angry, scared, sad, or happy, and how strong are those feelings on a scale of 1 to 10? In it you read, among other things, that the word emotion is linguistically related to motion! Our emotions are the sources of energy for movement in our lives. Emotion = motion! Suppressing (feelings) or letting them flow (energy) makes a big difference when it comes to exerting influence. Self-knowledge is also the beginning of wisdom here. Exploring your own emotional landscape and that of the organization in which you work provides insight into the possibilities for making a healthy use of the energy present in emotions.

We advise managers to create an (overall) feeling-o-gram for their organization. This provides the opportunity to explore the emotional landscape of the organization in more detail. We tell them to make sure there is space and time to discuss the feeling-o-gram with a number of colleagues if you wish. It works like this: make a kind of bar chart in which you indicate how much feeling you think the organization keeps inside and how much the organization brings out if there are the emotions of angry, scared, sad, and happy. And if there is displeasure or pleasure, how much (on a scale of 1 to 5) do they show of that, and how much of that do they keep to themselves?

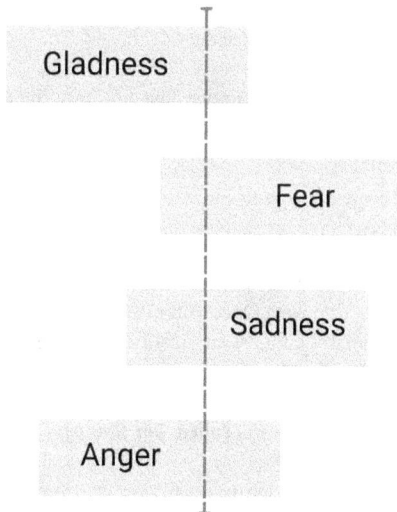

Figure 5.1 Feel-o-gram

Steiner is a great advocate of frank but controlled communication about feelings. This can give great results, especially if all interlocutors are willing to share their emotions.

Every human being, Steiner writes, makes emotional mistakes. Sometimes, we have little or no sense of what the other person is experiencing and how they are feeling. Then again, we become far too involved in the experiences of the other person and lose ourselves. As Aristotle said:

> [I]t is always about the right degree, the right moment, the right intention and in the right way. Where that fails, we all too easily end up in a psychological Game. We Persecute, we Rescue, or we play the helpless Victim. One of the reasons why people play a Game is, that this is how people attempt (unsuccessfully) to get positive strokes. This is an attempt that backfires. An attempt that actually produces negative strokes. The heart closes.
>
> (Goleman, 1996)

When you notice that you have ended up in such a Game, it is important, without getting defensive, to sincerely apologize for the emotional damage you have caused with your game-like behavior. This involves that:

- you admit to yourself that you made a mistake,
- you acknowledge your mistake to others,
- you have the realization that you are harming the other,
- you're feeling and conveying regret, and
- finally, you see that repair is necessary.

Anyone who dares to do so will notice that not only the air is cleared but also that a new reality is also emerging in which (emotional) issues can be discussed more easily.

Powerful phrases!

Positivity is an important and helpful choice if a manager wants to shape his self-control in an effective way. Once you make that choice as a manager, as a leader, and as a human being, being positive becomes a habit. Successful businessman and philanthropist Rich de Vos (1926–2018) gives an interesting example. He had a background in human relations. One of the books that he wrote on success in business is called *Ten Powerful Phrases for Positive People* (2008).

In his book, he introduces ten powerful phrases through which you can, looking forward, influence other people in a significant and positive way. The main and leading question in his life was: what's the next and best thing to do? Managers can learn a lot when they incorporate the following phrases in their daily behavior.

Although the ten phrases are quite simple and accessible (but far from simple to put into practice!), they can truly have an impact and can change behavior of our leaders.

The first two phrases are the most difficult. So . . . important to practice in real life!

1: I'm wrong.

If you're not able to express these words when you make a mistake, you will never be experienced as a true, authentic, and fair leader! It is namely the hardest thing to say, especially when power is on your side! By recognizing your own failures, you set a very important example toward people you work with. By being able to say I'm wrong!, you actually start a healing process.

2: I'm sorry!

This is a logical addition to the first phrase. When, as a manager, you are in power, it is probably easier to defend your opinion and position. Unfortunately, a lot of managers do. After all, your position is one up to your employees. Ask yourself what is fair to do, and, if necessary, don't hesitate to say frankly: I'm sorry!

These two are the most important and difficult phrases. Here are some others in a shortened version:

3. You can do it

You are a manager who encourages his employees and wants to take them to a next level and you really believe they can! Your encouragement has to be real, otherwise it is just plastic and fake.

4. I believe in you

You are a manager who has high expectations of the people (you yourself hired!) and are happy to work with them.

5. I'm proud of you

As a manager, you are in a Functional Parent ego state: you offer your employees the recognition they deserve and desire

6. Thank you!

Say no more!! Often, we only think these tiny phrases. But it's important to learn not only to think but mainly to communicate them. After all what is not explicitly communicated does not exist in real life.

7. I need you

As a manager, you realize that all the people who work so hard for the sake of the company have a need to feel needed. Don't only think about that: tell them!

8. I trust you!

Cooperation starts with the need for basic trust. Without trust, people will be reluctant to give their best. It just doesn't feel safe enough!

9. I respect you!

Respect is the heart of any successful relationship. See for more insights about the significance of respect in Chapter 4.

10. I love you

This phrase transcends and summarizes all other phrases!

Can you imagine that if, as a manager, you succeed in practicing these phrases in your behavior and in your way of communicating, you become powerful in the best way imaginable?

The Adult ego state

Those who have already read and learned more about Transactional Analysis will have noticed that the Adult I state has no subdivisions like the Parent and Child I states. TA is best known for the differentiation between the Critical Parent and the Nurturing Parent, the Adult and the Adapted Child and the Natural Child. The Adult usually remains 'empty'. A reaction from the Adult in the TA model of I states is a reaction to a here-and-now situation in which you use all the possibilities available to you as an adult human being. To properly distinguish your Adult behavior from your Parent and Child behavior, you can ask yourself: Was this behavior, thought, or feeling appropriate to the way an adult human being responds to what is going on at this moment? If your answer is 'yes', then your reaction is coming from your Adult I state.

Thinking about ego states within the TA has boomed in recent decades. In an effort to better understand how Eric Berne's powerful model works, much has been written precisely about the Adult ego state as well. When it comes to self-control as a source of influence and power, developing an optimally functioning Adult ego state is a condition sine qua non.

After all, the Adult ego state helps you stay alert, questioning, evaluating, grounded, and rational when the waves around you go high. You can apply these qualities of the Adult not only to the world around you. But also, just as importantly, for your inner world. When we are in our Adult ego state, we see the people around us as they are, without projecting all kinds of things onto them. We ask for information rather than remaining afraid or making assumptions. Therefore, the Adult is often recognizable by the open questions he asks: What do you mean? How did it happen? Where was it? Who said that? and so on. Of course, the Adult makes full use of the best stored in our Parent and in our Child. It is sometimes referred to in TA as the Integrating or Integrated Adult. In the model, the Adult is drawn in the middle for a reason. This shows that the Adult has the directing role when it comes to input from the world around us and from our inner world (Parent and Child). As mentioned, those who possess too little controlling ability (Adult) soon become victims of their own inner confusion and, in its wake, that of the outside world. This results in a corresponding loss of influence.

Talking about control: Abraham Lincoln

Abraham Lincoln, the 16th President of the United States, who endured the Civil War and abolished slavery despite personal tragedies and political opposition, was able to control himself well. He once said: 'Discipline is choosing between what you want now and what you want most' (quote by Abraham Lincoln: 'Discipline is choosing between what you want no . . .'; goodreads.com).

References

Armour, J.A. (2007) *The Little Brain on the Heart*, Cleveland Clinic Journal of Medicine, 74:Suppl 1, pp. S48–S51. https://doi.org/10.3949/ccjm.74. suppl_1

De Vos, R. (2008) *Ten Powerful Phrases for Positive People*. New York (NY): Centre Street.

Goleman, D. (1996) *Emotional Intelligence. Why It Can Matter More Than IQ*. London: Bloomsbury Publishing.

Steiner, C. (1996) *Emotional Literacy, Intelligence with a Heart*. Fawnskin (CA): Personhood Press.

Steiner, C.M. (1987) *The Seven Sources of Power: An Alternative to Authority*, TAJ, 17:3. https://doi.org/10.1177/036215378701700309

6 Communication

A limited possibility

A king once dreamed that all his teeth had fallen out. He sent for a fortune teller to explain the dream. In a pompous tone, this one said: 'Sire, your dream means that all your relatives will die and that you will be the only one left'. The king was seething at this explanation and ordered his servants to lock the soothsayer up on water and bread in the darkest dungeons under the palace. Then he sent for a second fortune teller. The latter heard the story and said thoughtfully: 'King, rejoice, for the dream means that you will live for many years to come. You will even outlive all your relatives. Long live the king!' The king was so pleased with this explanation that he tearfully embraced the soothsayer and gave him a large sum of money when he left.

Claude Steiner (1987) says of communication:

> The manager needs communication to impart knowledge, deal with prob-
> lems with others, and build and maintain fruitful relationships. Through
> the quality of his communication, he helps the other to develop a better
> understanding of the quality of product or service.

A very basic definition of communication is that it is an activity in which living beings exchange meanings by responding to each other's signals. A more complex view of communication can be found in Maturana (1984): 'Communication does not depend on what is being transferred, but on the person who undergoes it. And that is very different from "transferring information"'. It is clear that giving meaning is the core of communication. Giving meaning is, mind you, the prerogative of the recipient. So it is not about what the sender means but what the receiver makes of it.

Example: continuous use of terms such as change by management creates a high risk. On a macro level, change means we are going to change! On a micro level, this can easily take on the meaning of I'm falling short! In this way, the desired change in the minds and hearts of the employees does not come about. In terms of communication, change requires a more effective approach.

DOI: 10.4324/9781003452386-6

Too little or too much

Those who lack communicative power learn little. Lack of communication skills can lead to the manager not understanding the other person or being misunderstood himself.

This can lead to difficulty, or to misunderstanding, to confusion, misunderstandings (aware or even unaware), conflict, and even banal quarrels. If it escalates like this, the difference of opinion from business becomes very personal. In that case, it is almost impossible to turn back. So intervene in time! It is very important that the manager does not lose himself unnecessarily in clumsy communicative behavior. Problems in communication skills can manifest themselves in different ways. The biggest disaster is that no one takes the manager seriously anymore. The importance of effective communication cannot be overstated.

Those who overemphasize the role of communication become compulsive talkers, persuaders, and pastors of a bad sort. Companies and organizations now use, sometimes, huge numbers of communication consultants. Some CEOs make use of 14 full-time communications staff. The danger is that he and his story will disappear behind slick, slippery language that is more about manipulating than informing.

Linear causality

Thinking about communication is still strongly dominated by terms such as 'sending and receiving'. This is thinking in terms of linear causality. There is a stimulus and there is a response. There is one cause, and the rest is effect! However, once people are involved, linear causality no longer exists. There is then a circular coherence or better: an infinite cohesion. In communication, you often do not know where it starts and what the outcome, the result, depends on. In any case, the effect of communication is strongly influenced by meaning, which is colored by your gender, age, history, culture, and position. Humans are unique signifiers. In communication, therefore, there is always a question of 'subjective attribution of meaning to selective perception'. This makes communication not only fascinating but also complicated. One of the principles of the more systemic view of communication is: you do not understand communication by controlling it but by examining its limitations! After all, interpersonal relationships and communication are very complex phenomena. Those who are aware of the possibilities and impossibilities of human communication will better understand how influence can be optimally exercised.

TA is a powerful tool when it comes to a broader and deeper understanding of communicative (im)possibilities. Transactions are the building blocks of communication. Those who delve into the general aspects of communication (communication theory) and into the more personal characteristics of one's own communication (communication practice) can gain enormously in effectiveness in many areas of life, both private and at work. After all, it is through communication that you influence each other.

You cannot not have an impact

Influence is like the weather: it is always there. Whatever you say or do and also what you don't say or do will always bring a smile or a grimace. It is therefore valuable to think about the question: How do I come across? Or better: how do I want to come across? What effect am I aiming for, and am I succeeding? It is valuable in any communicative situation to always think about the question of which goal you are pursuing, short-term influence or longer-term influence.

An example: as long as a complaining customer is referred to as Mrs. Johnson, coordination, a good conversation, or reasonable consultation, is still possible. When we talk about 'that Johnson woman' at a later stage, we end up on the cutting edge of business and personal. By the time this customer is only referred to as 'That woman!', any prospect of agreement seems completely lost. Language matters!

Changing things purely on the basis of – usually hierarchical – power is effective at best in crisis situations. If, for example, a hospital is threatened with bankruptcy due to a financial shortfall, the crisis manager will have to intervene forcefully. The same is true in youth care, for example, because an abused young person must be placed out of the home immediately. Or a home situation is untenable: the demented elderly person must immediately be taken to crisis care. Or if a school has gotten such a bad name that parents no longer have any confidence in it. In these cases, disbanding and starting over can help.

In all other cases, such an approach leads only to very short-term change: fleeting and soon no longer significant. So, making changes on (autocratic) power is not useful if you want them to stick in the longer term. Also realize that people do want to change but do not want to be changed. This requires a careful and sustainable communicative approach, and that is a matter of patience. You can start with the first step and then proceed consistently to the finish line.

Important tool

'Ah', a nurse once said,

> I understand very well how management sees us. Recently, the director told me that the new strategic policy plan would place more responsibility

low down in the organization. That sounds nice as policy talk, but what I mostly hear is the word low. Low: that means my colleagues and me. Then they are obviously 'high'. Too bad, because I have always thought that our work with the patients is precisely the beating heart of the organization!

Language creates reality! The art is to use communication to influence the course of things. Perspective-rich interventions in language that bring all millimeter by millimeter closer to the dreamed reality.

So, what can you do? In everything we do, communication is the most important tool at our disposal. Everything is actually communication, and we can't do without it. It is crucial to use that tool as well and effectively as possible. Communication seldom provides a short-term, dead-bang effect, but there is a pleasant 'consolation': you can't not influence. To put it more perspectival: you always have influence. Admittedly a bit less spectacular than change management but more down-to-earth and with more understanding for the people who have to do the (real) work. We will have to think a little more along the lines of 'influence' rather than 'change', let alone 'change-management'. That kind of wording belongs to the manager, which is usually poorly understood on the shop floor. It is not wise, but rather undesirable, to assume that meanings are simply shared by sender and receiver. This kind of language eventually creates a linguistic distance, just like, for example: 'expertise', 'competencies', 'smart', 'performance', 'care product', 'large-scale interventions', 'customer value propositions', 'semi-tilted structure with matrix elements', etc.. Funny, even the word 'transparency' quickly acquires a veiled halo in certain circles of management.

The examples mentioned refer to a kind of meta-language, which in the long run also creates physical distance between people, especially between management and employees. And on a psychological level, unconsciously, that is probably the intention. Egos and status rise from the pan where principled commitment is out of the picture. In the public sector, that is the commitment of workers to the world of the citizen, the patient, and the learner. What is really needed is language that connects people and layers in organizations, that expresses commitment, and that is understood on the shop floor: at the heart of the organization.

Ego states

A key concept in Transactional Analysis (TA) is the concept of ego states. Eric Berne's practical and useful model for communication gives clear insight into what goes well communicatively between people and what could be improved. What does thinking differently about power, as we want to initiate in this book, mean when it comes to communication between people and between manager and employees? In that different approach, how do you use the five (ego state) options from TA: Critical Parent, Nurturing Parent, Adult,

Adapted Child, and Natural Child? Communicatively, it can make quite a difference which ego state is 'turned on'.

Is one better and more appropriate than the other or does it depend mostly on the situation which is best? The Parent ego state tells others what to do and what is acceptable and not acceptable, nurturing, or critical. The Adult ego state thinks logically and acts rationally, making the best possible decisions according to the rules of logic. The Child ego state is adapted under the influence of the Critical Parent or spontaneously supported and encouraged by the Nurturing Parent. The main function of the Critical Parent is to (safely) direct others. Here lies, if not careful, the source par excellence of power games and abuse of power. The Critical Parent is a coherent, learned set of critical and directing and controlling positions. 'This is the way to do it' However, the Critical Parent not only directs others. But also this ego state keeps us, if we are not careful, under it in the same way. Autonomy, disobedience, and freedom depend on how far the influence of the Critical Parent extends. How much power do we give the critical voice in ourselves and the critical voices of others? Everyone has and needs a Critical Parent in everyday life. How far its influence extends varies from person to person. When the Critical Parent speaks to us 'from within', his basic message is quite often: 'You are not OK! That power in its old, familiar (?) Critical Parent sense (control of many by few) is ineffective in the long run, leads to uninspiring adaptation and undermines any creativity, is nicely illustrated by the following story about a group of lumberjacks.

A group of lumberjacks is tasked with cutting down a fixed number of square meters of forest each day. Headquarters keeps a close eye on the production figures. Soon production is in steep decline. It becomes so worrisome that the director decides to travel to the forest area. Once there, it turns out that the declining production is caused by the saws and axes becoming blunt. The director says: 'Then don't you take them to the blacksmith to have them sharpened? The jacks reply deadly serious: 'No, you can't, because then we won't make our production!'

Managers who handle power differently especially invite their employees to think for themselves! They know that their 'lumberjacks' are not just cutting down trees but are themselves thinking about what is needed in a broader sense to achieve a good result.

Nonverbal?

Since Mehrabian's 1967 study, much has been said and written about the role nonverbal utterances play in communication as a whole. In many management courses, it is still taught that Mehrabian claimed that 55 percent of communication is visual (body language such as posture and gestures), 38 percent vocal (tone, loud or soft), and 7 percent verbal (content). According to this analysis, 93 percent of communication is nonverbal. For years, it has been argued that it is not about what you say, but how you say it. Of course, the how is a significant factor.

However, Mehrabian's research mainly focused on what happens when people communicate with each other about their feelings. In that case, nonverbal communication is dominant. When it comes to a business, content exchange, the content becomes more important. Moreover, much research after 1967 (including Burgoon et al., 1996) shows that the context also has an enormous influence on the question of what role nonverbal factors play. Who says what, where, and when? Whether as a manager you casually ask an employee at the end of a working day how things are going at home or whether you do so in a conversation to which you invited the employee separately can make a big difference. The meaning of your question will be perceived differently, and you will probably get a different answer.

Encouraging and enriching language

Communication is a transactional process. Following Eric Berne (YouTube: www.youtube.com/watch?v=eLQS0IxLYMg, accessed on September 4, 2023), we use the word 'transactional' instead of 'interactional', because the word transaction shows that communication is always about investment and return. You depend, for the success of your communication, on the 'other side'. It will not work without the other's benevolence and listening ear. Your interlocutor will interpret everything you say in terms of his own internal structure. He/she cannot do otherwise. The same applies to yourself. In the complexity of sending and receiving, speaking, and listening, one exchanges information, creates new knowledge, solves problems, and builds relationships. Communication is the most effective in conjunction with the other sources of influence mentioned in this book. All these sources from which we can draw power work together, if all goes well, flawlessly.

Contemporary views on communication are strongly influenced by thinking from modern biology perspective. There it is assumed that a cell, an organism (and therefore an organization!) are half-open and half-closed systems. This system can open and close at will. It determines for itself what it lets in or what it excludes. Tearing open or slamming shut from the outside is not an option. Pure power only has the effect of the organism 'choosing' to close. Only the benevolence of the organism determines whether the cell opens or closes. The phenomenon of communication does not depend on what is being transmitted but rather on the person who undergoes it. And, according to Maturana and Varela in 'The tree of knowledge' (1984) that is quite different from transferring information.

The teacher grumbles to his colleague, 'Then I want them to come up with an answer and all are silent. That pisses me off so much!' Anyone who would look through the keyhole of the classroom would see how the 24 'cells' in their benches have closed completely, probably as early as entering the room.

A logical system

From this thinking from biology perspective, every human being is a logical system (Adler, 1998). A person's view of an issue is logical in this view. Not according to the laws of logic but according to its own origins and reasons. If the system closes itself to the influences from the outside world, this is, reasoned from the system itself, perfectly logical. Even if it opens up, it has good reasons for doing so. The consequence of all this is the view that you cannot change another person but can only provide material that makes it possible for the other person to change himself. Communication is one of the most important tools of managers here. The organization by which living beings are defined is called an autopoietic (self-realizing) organization. Autopoiesis is the mechanism, which makes living beings autonomous systems. When two people interact, they create a social link. There is mutual involvement in the realization of everyone's autopoiesis.

So, the most important question for the one who leads – the teacher, the manager, the director – is not: what do I think about it? But: can I make sense of it? After all, an opinion is nothing more than a subjective attribution of a selective perception. Opinions have a limited shelf life. Goethe (1766–1832) already advised in his time, '*Nicht ärgern, nur wundern*'. (Don't be angry, just be amazed.) Wonder, questioning, curiosity: wasn't that the path Einstein took so successfully? If, as a manager, you let go of the need to change (them), if you can temporarily park your opinion for a moment, if you don't get annoyed but rather wonder, then a new perspective emerges. It doesn't get easier, but it does get more exciting! And more promising . . . Then you will also see that not only a person, but also an organization, is not a make-able world that can be changed with power and force. Then you will see that there is no alternative to the laborious search for opportunities to influence. As said: that influence is always there, sometimes almost imperceptibly and every now and then illuminating and offering perspective.

Creating your reality

Communication is much more than language. Still, it is important to look carefully at the words we use. A few examples:

- A mayor says in a coaching conversation about his municipality, 'It's a snake pit here!'
- A director asks a training agency, 'Do you have a course on dealing with difficult employees?'
- During the meeting, within three minutes, the instructors come to the conclusion: 'Ahmed is lazy and unmotivated'.
- A consultant who wants to implement a major change comes to the conclusion: 'The team is completely in resistance!'

- On one news channel, people talk enthusiastically about the successes of the resistance fighters. On another channel, the same people are called terrorists.

This way of looking, like the accompanying choice of words, is completely ineffective. It detracts from a reality that is considerably more complex. Apparently, people take advantage of presenting things that way. What benefit do you see? Most perpetrators are also victims, and most transgressions involve a multitude of people. Once people are involved, linear causality does not exist!

Language creates reality! What makes this way of looking at things and this choice of words ineffective? How does this detract from a much more complex reality? What benefit do people get from phrasing things this way?

The purpose of managerial communication is perhaps above all to encourage people. That is literally to provide courage. This is best done through enriching interventions. As a manager, you can play an excellent role in this: with words, conversations, and moments of consultation with which people do not leave (an illusion) poorer but richer. This contributes to their self-image and increases their self-confidence, which, after all, is the fundamental floor on which we all stand. Invest in the quality of the encounter! An honest 'exchange' in communication is in any case: mutual acknowledgment of the obvious effort and a communicative reflection on perceived disadvantage.

Talking about communication: Ronald Reagan

Former US president Ronald Reagan was known as the Great Communicator. His speeches, in favor of political conservatism, illustrate the power of effective presidential communication. Reagan did not see himself as a great communicator: 'I never thought it was my style or the words I use that made a difference. It was the content. I wasn't a great communicator, but I communicated great things' (www.reaganlibrary.gov/archives/speech/farewell-address-nation). Well . . .

References

Adler, A. (1998, first publication 1927) *Understanding Human Nature*. Center City (MN): Hazelden Foundation.

Burgoon, J.K., Buller, D.B. and Woodall, W.G. (1996) *Nonverbal Communication: The Unspoken Dialogue*. New York (NY): McGraw-Hill.

Maturana, H.R. and Varela, F.J. (1984) *The Tree of Knowledge: The Biological Roots of Human Understanding*. Boston (MA): Shambala.

Mehrabian, A. (1971) *Silent Messages*. Belmont: Wadsworth.

Steiner, C.M. (1987) *The Seven Sources of Power: An Alternative to Authority*, TAJ, 17:3. https://doi.org/10.1177/036215378701700309

7 Information

Enough is enough?

A fisherman found in his net a bottle with a cork on it. When he removed the cork, to his surprise a genie appeared. The freed spirit told the fisherman that he could make three wishes. The fisherman thought deeply and replied: 'I would like you to grant me wisdom. That will help me make a right choice for the other wishes'. 'It has already happened', said the spirit, 'What are your next wishes? The fisherman thought for a moment and, becoming wise, said, 'Thank you. I have no further wishes'.

Claude Steiner (1987) says of information as a source of influence: 'In the past, knowledge was power. Now those who know how to find the right information increase their ability to influence' (https://begrippen.archixl.nl/archixl/nl/pageInformatie?clang=nl, approached on June 22, 2023). Information is anything that adds knowledge and thus reduces ignorance, uncertainty, or indeterminacy. No manager wants to be seen as ignorant, insecure, and indecisive. The demand for knowledge and information is a more difficult question for many managers than they thought before they started the job. Sometimes, it's good to say, like the fisherman in the story: Enough is enough! Or not . . . ?

Too little or too much

The manager who lacks information is ignorant. The Dutch Railways has been led for many years by a CEO who had no knowledge and experience whatsoever with regard to the technology of the rail company. Niente. Nada. This led to disastrous decisions and major loss of assets. Apparently, corporate decision-makers still assume that the director does not need to understand the product or the production processes. Ignorant but ambitious managers made rash mergers,

DOI: 10.4324/9781003452386-7

were fooled by smart talkers, and played the great financial wizard with the well-known consequences. Good knowledge and information management is an important weapon in the fight against waste. Lack of knowledge and information costs money. There is a strong relationship between the level of knowledge in the organization and the costs of failure. Studies (www.iseeiknow.com/posts/whitepaper-kennis-kwaliteit, approached on June 7, 2023) show that, depending on the industry, no less than 3 to 15 percent of turnover is wasted on failure costs.

It is not always useful to have more information than is usual or strictly necessary. The overinformed manager too easily behaves as a kind of hyperintellectual, creating distance to the shop floor. Of course, it may also indicate that the manager is overqualified for the job. The question remains: Which information and in what quantity do you need to make the right decision? And then again: What information in what amount do you need to provide this question with a good answer? And so forth.

Wisdom of crowds

Wisdom requires not only deep insight but also the broadest possible, realistic view of reality as it presents itself to you. Acting wisely is a difficult task for a person on his own. On your own, you only have a limited field of vision. As organizations become more complex and the social context more turbulent, it is all the more desirable to make use of a multitude of people with different views. This is called diversity. The manager who made Google great, Eric Schmidt, was and is very clear about this. He wants to have nothing to do with a team in which everyone has the same information and holds the same opinions. Schmidt is someone who seeks to have dissent. He emphatically invites the members of his team to speak out. Especially if they have different information or a different opinion. Many employees, especially at executive level, are afraid to speak out. Schmidt suspended decision-making when he felt that a multitude of perspectives were not available. He wanted and still wants to use the wisdom of crowds (www.youtube.com/watch?v=wPHL4paHv0o, approached on June 7, 2023).

Differences in expertise, work style, temperament, gender, seniority, and outlook ensure that the complementary team of managers together can cover and oversee the broad spectrum of all issues at hand. Diversity, dissent, and complementarity provide additional opportunities for optimal results. All noses in different directions (to see the whole playing field), but with the same goal in mind. The team of managers who are able to connect information, experience, intuition, and vision prove to be the most influential and charismatic. Even at the individual level, it is important for a manager to unite these things within himself as well as possible. These are aspects that each have their own validity and add something essential to the personal power of each manager.

Crucial information

Manager and information relate like rider and horse. The rider uses all the horse's abilities and qualities to achieve his goal. The rider leads the horse, not the other way around. Information is crucial to good management. Key figures, indicators, trends, market developments, and ratios all belong to the complex information domain of the manager. Having good and reliable information helps the manager to influence and guide vision and plans. Without that information, the manager is ignorant, and his actions will eventually be justifiably labeled as naive. Some things you have to, depending on the type of organization you work for, just know or know how to find:

- What is in the corporate or multiyear plan and are we doing what we agreed to do?
- Are we doing the right things and are we doing the right things well?
- How are we doing financially? What are the prospects?
- What trends are recognizable in our market or field?
- What is the personnel situation: growth rates, absenteeism, performance, and evaluation, etc.?
- How do our customers value our products and services?
- How about the number of customer contacts? Quotations? Orders?

And after each answer invariably comes the final question: What significance does this information have for the functioning of our organization or corporation?

Of course, without wishing to turn the manager into the old all-knowing know-it-all, the aforementioned list of necessary 'facts' can be extended considerably. Therein lies at the same time the risk, the distortion, of the quality called information. The danger is lurking if a manager spends all day managing with figures, preferably behind the computer. In this way he becomes detached from his core task: his own inspiration and involvement with the people he serves and for whom he is responsible. After all, this is the apparent paradox of being a manager: service and responsibility.

If a 20 percent cutback means that in a nursing home, the existing standard of holding a dying person's hand for five minutes a day is adjusted downwards to four minutes, then that is an enormous result in figures, but an indigestible loss in quality. In this way, quality is eroded by a one-sided rational view of market and efficiency thinking. The horse has bolted and takes the rider with him in his mad flight. It seems so obvious: without inspiration, information becomes cold manipulation. But equally true: without numbers, inspiration becomes vague spirituality. The following story shows how a supposedly efficient manager can completely overshoot the mark.

A manager had received free tickets to a performance of Schubert's Unfinished Symphony from his director. The next day, he wrote his director a memo with his findings:

- The four oboists had nothing to do for a very long time. Their share could easily be divided among the rest of the orchestra.
- All 12 violinists played the same notes. This leads to unnecessary duplication.
- There is no need for the horns to repeat all the passages already played by the string instruments.
- If all superfluous passages were deleted, the concerto could be reduced to four minutes.

If Schubert had kept to this, he could have just finished his 8th symphony. Don't leave composing to managers!

The Little Professor

Many TA professionals, following Eric Berne (1964), speak of intuition as The Little Professor. A nice way to upgrade this human potential. The word intuition comes from Latin and literally means 'seeing within'. By intuition, most people mean something other than the rational thinking mind. It is about standing still, feeling, and spontaneously 'knowing', without concrete reasoning. The subdivision of the Adult ego state within the Child ego state (A1), the Little Professor, is especially committed to survival, having to figure out the best way to maintain the bond with parental figures while trying to get rid of the injunctions given by these same figures. A1 is a naive and astute 'adult' who seeks to change reality to meet basic needs, with resources being intuition, Martian thinking, and fantasy (Caetano Alves, 2019). This ability remains available for a lifetime. Here too, the following applies: use it or lose it.

It's clear, information alone won't get you there. Managers who get no further than 'measuring is knowing' forget that that flat slogan was invented long ago in the United States to keep third-rate managers in check. In his book *Modern Capitalism*, Donald Kalff (2009) talks about utopian rationalism in this context: the idea that only on the basis of rational management techniques you can realize God's kingdom on earth. A fable! It takes more than that. Like intuition for the right course and the right decision. By far, most of our knowing is feeling. Did you know that intuition is also referred to as automated knowledge? In our opinion, managers make too little use of this and rely mainly on what the conscious mind produces, such as numerical support in management report and other nice things. And that while the environment is VUCA: volatile, uncertain, complex, and ambivalent. This puts all figures in perspective, especially if they are to provide a perspective for the future. But it is literally unpredictable and unreliable when it comes to foreseeing what is about to happen. On a global scale, this is evident time and again. Who saw the September 11 attacks coming, the war in Ukraine, the impact of AI, and more?

Peter Senge (2006) emphasizes that the consequences of managers' decisions in a turbulent context are limited. And yet, do we cling desperately to numbers? It seems better to see the figures as a pleasant support in complex decisions! Should we still trust our intuition? Decisions made by your subconscious mind are often the best, according to psychologist Ap Dijksterhuis (2015). In his book *Het Slimme Onbewuste* (The Clever Unconscious), he provides many proofs that unconscious decision-making often leads to a considerably better result. Intuition is the first inspiration that comes to mind when an issue arises.

The unconscious is the smart big brother (or sister) of the conscious. Reason enough to rely on it some more. According to senior psychologist Dijksterhuis, the unconscious is actually much more objective than the conscious. The unconscious can process as much as two hundred thousand times more information than the conscious. Our conscious mind just hops along behind it. The power of genes of a brain that has evolved over the centuries, experiences in the backward part of life, and intensive social intercourse with others are partly responsible for our sensitivity. Our unconscious is, in the words of Wilhelm Wundt (1874), the founder of empirical psychology, an unknown person who creates and produces for us and eventually throws the ripe fruit into our lap like this. The unconscious seeks and offers the answer. The conscious accepts it gratefully – without knowing where it comes from. Although Wundt later abandoned his early theory of the unconscious, it makes you think.

How can you learn to use that unconscious better? By incorporating moments of rest more often: sleeping, meditating, walking the dog, gardening, and anything else that allows the mind to run free. Then the unconscious goes to work, arranging, ranking, and linking. Rest advances reflection. It is necessary for the brain to neurologically fiddle with past experiences. When making the next decision, that vast source of knowledge can then provide good, free advice.

Words, words, words?

A rich man saw a fisherman lying lazily beside his boat. 'Why aren't you fishing?' he asked. 'Because I have caught enough for today', replied the fisherman. 'I have a different vision. If you catch more, you could make more money. You could then buy a motorboat and go farther out to sea to catch even more fish. And you could buy nylon nets to catch bigger fish. Then you'd buy another boat and maybe someday you'd have a whole fleet. Then you could be rich like me and really start enjoying your life!' 'Then what do you think I am doing now?' replied the fisherman.

Mission, vision, and strategy are words that are used in a variety of contexts in a variety of meanings. Therefore, we begin here with some clarification.

- Mission says something about the raison d'être of an organization. That is the basis of our existence! That is what we do it for! That is why mission is not always up for discussion.
- Vision says something about looking to the future. Vision has its own, unquantifiable evidence. Vision is the image of the desirable future. So, there is also an element of dreaming in it.
- Strategy should make those dreams, that future, a reality and describes all the actions needed to realize the vision. Strategy is consistent and is also not subject to constant change.

As a manager, you really ought to know what the mission of your organization is. And its vision. You should also have an idea how vision and mission relate to reality on a scale of 0 to 10. Is it only words, words, words or are these clear texts that are recognizable in what people really do and experience in the heart of the organization? Most of all, in communication with employees, it is important to realize that strategy should be presented as a temptation, not as an assault.

What does mission and vision mean on a personal level? First of all, it is important that you can sufficiently identify with especially the mission and vision of the organization you work for. If not, there are always the three choices you also encountered in Chapter 1:

- Accept that it is the way it is.
- Change what you think you can change.
- Saying goodbye if neither of these options work for you.

Accepting a dream that is not your dream is easier for some than others. Adapting to it becomes easier if you can manage to confine yourself to your 'circle of influence'. So don't complain and whine either, but loyally make your personal contribution.

Change is also a possibility. You can change yourself, of course, and tweak your dream a bit so that it fits better into the bigger picture. You can also get your surroundings to move. You do understand that this requires you to come up with a good 'story', to be convincing and inspiring, and to have the facts on your side. This is not an easy road . . . and again, complaining and whining are not options. Great changes have sometimes come about because someone somewhere had the courage to take their dream seriously enough.

Saying goodbye is the last option, if accepting and changing turn out to be dead-end paths for you. Start looking for a dream that does suit you. But make sure you can leave with your head held high. This is possible if you have made your contribution as a professional to the best of your ability. Again, complaining and whining are not options.

Everyone weaves their own thread in the great tapestry of the organization where you work. Your thread partly colors the great tapestry. That's where your influence is, and under the influence of your thread, the tapestry also changes. If you have dabbled and struggled enough, but remained dissatisfied with the outcome, then it might be time to leave or adapt.

MWP and AI

We suspect that the possibilities offered by Artificial Intelligence (AI) will drastically change the manager's work. The way in which the manager collects information and makes decisions will be strongly altered by AI. Computers can simply process a much larger amount of data at a much faster pace. AI management is a growing and changing field that presents many opportunities and challenges for managers across all industries and functions. The impact of AI on almost all processes in a company or organization is increasing rapidly and with it the urgency to formulate a strategy based on this. Managers must be aware of the possibilities and limitations of AI and be prepared to continuously adapt and learn in a world of smart machines. As with all knowledge, the power that knowledge brings can be used for good or evil.

Talking about information: Angela Merkel

The former chancellor of Germany, Angela Merkel, was known for always appearing well-informed at the consultation table. She was even thoroughly informed about side issues: 'I am not an expert in this field, but I do try to keep up to date with the Bundesliga. And I do follow World Cups and European Championships more closely'. She knew what she needed to know before talking about anything (www.brainyquote.com/quotes/angela_merkel_326167).

References

Berne, E. (1964) *Games People Play, The Psychology of Human Relationships*. New York (NY): Grove Press.

Caetano Alves, T. (2019) *The Little Professor: Reflection on the Structure, Development and Evolution of the Adult in the Child*, International Journal of Transactional Analysis, 10:2, pp. 79–86. https://doi.org/10.29044/v10i2p79

Dijksterhuis, A. (2015) *Het Slimme Onbewuste, Denken met Gevoel (The Clever Unconsciousness, Thinking with Feeling)*. Amsterdam: Prometheus/Bert Bakker.

Kalff, D. (2009) *Modern Kapitalisme, Alternatieve Grondslagen voor Grote Ondernemingen (Modern Capitalism, Alternative Foundations for Large Corporations)*. Amsterdam: Business Contact.

Senge, P. (2006) *The Fifth Discipline, The Art & Practice of the Learning Organization*. London: Crown Pub.

Steiner, C.M. (1987) *The Seven Sources of Power: An Alternative to Authority*, TAJ, 17:3. https://doi.org/10.1177/036215378701700309

Wundt, W. (1874) *Grundzüge der Physiologischen Psychologie (Fundamentals of Physiological Psychology)*. Leipzig: Wilhelm Engelmann.

8 Transcendence

The right thing at the right moment

The do-gooder was tired, and the world had not yet improved. He decided to pay another visit to his teacher, who lived in a cottage on the shore of a large lake. He hoped that visit would give him new ideas. The master received him on the veranda of his house, offered him a chair, and put on hot water for tea. After listening to his pupil's complaint, he was silent for a while as if waiting for what was to come. Then he stood up, took a scoop of tea leaves, walked to the edge of the lake, and threw the leaves into the water. Very briefly, some of the water colored, but the color soon disappeared into the larger body of water. Then, he scooped a spoonful of tea leaves into a cup and poured water on it. The water turned a reddish-brown color and had a pleasant smell. The master took a sip of tea and said: 'A large lake cannot be changed by one spoonful, a cup of water can'.

Claude Steiner says of transcendence: 'Here it is about the ability to take distance and let things run their course without getting confused. Those who realize what life is really about, remain calm in the midst of a hectic environment'.

Of all the sources of power, this is probably the one with the strangest look and feel. It is as if Steiner advises managers to leave things alone. How can that ever be a source of power and influence? The more one takes the time to absorb this initially strange advice, the more one will understand its meaning. You can only keep something if you dare to lose it, you can only hold on if you dare to let go.

Too much, too little

People whose capacity for transcendence is underdeveloped see themselves as the center of events. They cling to (personal) beliefs and needs. People with narcissistic personality disorder for instance think

---

DOI: 10.4324/9781003452386-8

they are better than others. They exhibit selfish behavior, are dominant, want to be admired, and often lack empathy. People with narcissistic personality disorder consider themselves more important than others.

Too much transcendence produces detachment, a strong relativization of 'earthly matters', drifting away from what matters here-and-now. These people need to be reminded regularly that life is only now. Your life is never not in the now. The only place you can ever encounter the future is in your head. The same goes for the past.

Vacation?

Some young international entrepreneurs are experimenting with the strategy of 'taking a leave of absence' when their business is in rough waters. Taking a break seems an odd action when the motto seems to be 'all hands-on-deck'. It is almost unheard of; it seems like an escape from taking responsibility. Recall, however, that the word 'vacation' has its roots in the Latin *vacare*, meaning 'to be free from' or 'to be free for'. This ultimate letting go, this search for 'rest', literally taking distance allows them to 'let things run their course more'. This requires trust in the power of systems' self-healing ability.

A different perspective often leads to new insights. By consciously gaining new experiences, these CEOs notice that more and more possibilities are unfolding. You could say that they temporarily exchange the field perspective (two-dimensional) for the observation perspective (three-dimensional). It is often a choice to see things differently and to have an open attitude.

This of course cannot be the advice to captains to abandon the sinking ship. Sometimes it is necessary to rise above a given situation (and perhaps also above yourself), Steiner seems to be saying. In this chapter, we explore some recent management ideas related to this line of thinking.

During the first decade of this century, the belief (!) that the future is socially engineerable was increasingly questioned. Doubts arose around the beliefs 'sold' by success gurus: If it's to be, it's up to me! In itself, of course, this is not nonsense. How your life and work turn out is certainly influenced by the choices you make. The screaming success gurus with their slogans like 'Success is a choice!' and 'The future is not what's going to happen. The future is what you will do!' have also found the end of their rightness, however, it seems. The injustice (It's just not true!) and the unmercifulness (It's also a rock-hard lie!) of such one-liners make one busily search for what then does determine the course of things. You'll just see ball 88 roll out of the lottery ball in front of you where 'ball 88' stands for 'bad luck' and 'stupid bad luck'. The period of postmodernity that lies behind us has taught us, in any case, that there is no one truth and that different perspectives can coexist.

In itself, taking personal responsibility is of course a fine thing. However, the reality in which we live and work is a bit too complex to hang the course of things entirely on it.

Presencing

More often, we should (dare to) let things take their course, and that is quite in line with what contemporary management prophets examine as a possible passable path. Such luminaries as Peter Senge, Joseph Jaworski, and Otto Scharmer (2009), who have each individually earned their spurs in management land, are discussing new so-called paradigms. A paradigm is 'a coherent system of models and theories that form a perspective through which "reality" is analyzed and described'. Old paradigms in which the future seemed to be mainly the result of all decisions people made no longer seem to be adequate. In their equally beautiful and confusing book *Presence*, Senge, Jaworski, Scharmer, and Betty Sue Flowers are together in search of new paradigms. The concept of presencing represents the special moment when people dare to let go of their fixed patterns of thinking, their feelings, and even their aspirations, creating the space for substantially new insights.

Anyone who thought they could exert power and influence by making all kinds of decisions about the future of their organization was firmly knocked back by Jaap Boonstra (2000) at the beginning of this century. In one of his first lectures as a professor of change management, he began with the sobering sentence:

> Over 70 percent of change processes in Dutch organizations get bogged down prematurely or do not achieve the intended results. Customers notice nothing of the announced improvements, policy does not get off the ground, objectives are not achieved, and employees and managers lose track.

Should a manager from outside our country still harbor illusions, Boonstra dashes those hopes with the statement that 'the high percentage of stalled change processes corresponds with experiences in the outside world'. If anyone interested in Boonstra's analysis, we would like to refer to his booklet *Walking on Water*. Our concern is to at least put central concepts from contemporary management paradigms such as power, influence, and social engineering in perspective.

Over the years, we have learned that there are two reflection questions that cannot be skipped: What should you have done that you did not do? And what did you not do that you should have done? You too have probably experienced less or completely unsuccessful change processes in your organization. How do you look back on them? In your opinion, what is the root cause of this failure?

The boiled frog

The foursome who marketed the book *Presence* question a good deal of old wisdom. They also make a plea to be especially curious about new insights. What is their point? Most learning theories focus on reflection of the past. People are mostly inclined to look at specific situations and simple problems that call for a (rather successful) standard solution. In organizations, this leads to what Senge once called (2012) the parable of the boiled frog. Put a frog in a pan of boiling water, and it jumps out as quickly as possible. Put a frog in a pan of cold water on a low heat, however, and it will stay put until it is boiled to death.

Behavior in organizations is mainly determined by habits. People do what they have always done. They assume that Einstein was right that if you do what you always did, you will get what you always got. In a system in which complementary transactions have long dominated the existing culture, it is daring to throw in a cross-transaction. You are perceived as a spoilsport, as someone who sets aside the (usually unrealized) agreements. When a nurse in a healthcare institution where requests for help are always met sympathetically suddenly responds with, 'How about rolling up your sleeves yourself?', she is quickly seen as an obstructionist. Organizations and the people who work in them become attached to old, once successful practices. When the environment, the world in which they do business, changes, many organizations fail to notice this in time. Learning is mainly reactive: the world is viewed from familiar perspectives and models. Interpretations of reality that are different are easily disqualified. It is therefore not out of the question that some readers may not even read this sentence because they have already dropped out on reading 'such nonsense'.

The world we live and work in has many characteristics of a labyrinth. It is volatile, uncertain, complex, and ambivalent: VUCA! One thing is certain however: overly simplistic maps only prolong the time we spend wandering. The authors of *Presence* suggest that we need to fundamentally change our view of reality. The ego's view prevents us humans from coming into deep connection with the whole system. Viewing reality from the whole, from the interconnectedness of things, creates a transformation of consciousness, they argue. Managers then come into a different kind of connection with their environment. So, it is about the capacity to 'listen deeper and be open to new things'. Existing identities, need for control, prejudgments, and historical ways of thinking and acting can then be let go of. This enables people to get a grip on what is developing in the future and to create and shape fundamentally new ideas.

Unexpected and surprising

The power of the unexpected and the influence of the surprising might be greater than we suspect. It is just the question whether we are shaping the future with all our deciding. Perhaps we are getting in the way of the future? A step aside, a step back, or at least a more open and receptive attitude allows the future to unfold. The future may not be what we are going to do at all, the message seems to be. The future is what is going to happen. A little less hassle makes things a lot easier for the future to happen!

We started this book with a wink by asking you, following an experience of Albert Einstein, the following question: Does power even work if you don't believe in it? Perhaps that is the most important question you can ask when it comes to power. In any case, our script beliefs are that what you believe about yourself, others, and the world you live and work in. They have a major impact on how you handle your own and others' power. The good news is: they are just beliefs. Change can come in two different ways: we can change the world around us or we can change the way we see it by changing the world within!

Unleash the powers

After learning about Henry Mintzberg's book *Managers, not MBAs* (2004), we became even more concerned about the increasing popularity of these MBA courses. In short, Mintzberg's concern boils down to this: the conventional MBA classrooms overemphasize the science of management while ignoring the art of it and belittling the craft, creating a distorted view of the practice. We need to go back to a more engaged management style, to build stronger organizations, not inflated stock prices. This calls for a different approach to management training, where practicing managers learn from their own experience. We need to build the art and craft back into management education and into management itself.

Most managers believe that their employees are their most important asset. We like to believe that and agree with them that employees can make a difference. However, if we then start a discussion of questions about the development and functioning of people, it quickly falls silent. There is (still) too little knowledge of (developmental) psychology among managers. Fortunately, this is turning. Courses that open up the field of psychology to managers can look forward to an increase in the number of participants.

One of the encouraging voices in this area comes from US professor George Kohlrieser. In a seminar (2017), he once asked the following intriguing question to the managers present: 'Have you ever been guided by someone who cared about you like family and challenged you to achieve more than you ever thought possible for yourself, your organization and even society?' With *Care to Dare* (2012), Kohlrieser emphasizes that the task of the manager is to challenge his employees to deliver good performance *and* to 'take care' of them: to give sincere attention, to really listen, and to maintain an emotional connection in addition to content. In his book *Hostage at the Table*, he contends that conflict resolution is not difficult if we understand how human self-esteem operates. He believes that deep within humans reside slumbering powers that most of us do not even activate. These latent powers can revolutionize our lives if aroused and put into action. Kohlrieser's view completes the circle of this book. We count the seven sources of power we wrote about (motivated by Claude Steiner) among these latent powers Kohlrieser writes about. It's time to unleash these powers.

Talking about transcendence: Eckhart Tolle

The German teacher and author in the field of spirituality has his own view on the power of letting go. He says: 'Sometimes letting things go is an act of far greater power than defending them or hanging on to them' (Tolle, 2006). A nice appeal at the end of a book in which many thoughts about 'power' have been shared. Letting them go can be an act of power.

References

Boonstra, J. (2000) *Lopen Over Water. Over dynamiek van organiseren, vernieuwen en leren* (*Walking on Water. About Dynamics of Organizing, Innovation and Learning*). Amsterdam: UvA.

Kohlrieser, G. (2006) *Hostage at the Table: How Leaders Can Overcome Conflict, Influence Others, and Raise Performance*. Hoboken (NJ): Jossey-Bass.

Kohlrieser, G. (2012) *Care to Dare: Unleashing Astonishing Potential Through Secure Base Leadership*. Hoboken (NJ): Jossey-Bass.

Mintzberg, H. (2004) *Managers, Not MBAs. A Hard Look at the Soft Practice of Managing and Management Development*. Oakland (CA): Berrett-Koehler Publishers.

Senge, P.M., Scharmer, C.O., Flowers, B.S, Jaworski, J. (2005) *Presence: Exploring Profound Change in People, Organizations and Society*. Hachette: Nicholas Brealey Publishing.

Steiner, C.M. (1987) *The Seven Sources of Power: An Alternative to Authority*, TAJ, 17:3. https://doi.org/10.1177/036215378701700309

Tolle, E. (2006) *A New Earth: Awakening to Your Life's Purpose*. New York (NY): Plume.

Index

Note: Page numbers in *italics* indicate a figure on the corresponding page.